The
Cottage Fairy
Companion

The
Cottage Fairy
Companion

A Cottagecore Guide to Slow Living,
Connecting to Nature, and Becoming
Enchanted Again

Paola Merrill

yellow pear press

CORAL GABLES

For permission requests, please contact the publisher at:
Mango Publishing Group
2850 S Douglas Road, 4th Floor
Coral Gables, FL 33134 USA
info@mango.bz

For special orders, quantity sales, course adoptions and corporate sales, please email the publisher at sales@mango.bz. For trade and wholesale sales, please contact Ingram Publisher Services at customer.service@ingramcontent.com or +1.800.509.4887.

The Cottage Fairy Companion: A Cottagecore Guide to Slow Living, Connecting to Nature, and Becoming Enchanted Again

Library of Congress Cataloging-in-Publication number: 2022937417
ISBN: (print) 978-1-64250-979-3, (ebook) 978-1-64250-980-9
BISAC category code HOM023000, HOUSE & HOME / Small Spaces

Printed in the United States of America

To all who have supported me on this journey, online and in person.
Thank you. And for the valley I call home, where it all began.

Contents

Introduction

A Bit About Me

I came to the valley in June. It was a quiet place, nestled in the foothills of the Cascade Mountains.

The balsamroot had recently gone to seed, and the hillsides were fading from a rich green to the soft browns and yellows of a full summer. I'd come to know the seasons quite well over the next several years. Much of it would be a thorough study conducted through the bedroom window of my cottage, where I would sit at my desk and work nearly every day. As I painted or wrote, my eyes regularly checked the view, seeking the curious little moments that revealed some intimate detail about the ever-changing landscape.

From that window, I would see my first moose cow, leading her trembling newborn to the lakeside a half mile's trek down the road. Six months later, the frigid clear skies on a winter's night, dappled with the brightest clusters of stars I had ever seen. Yet the most rewarding moment by far would be spying a diminutive bluebell growing by my garden fence. It peeped through the chilled ground, a harbinger of spring when my world seemed so still and unrelentingly cold.

My cottage and I share an intimacy likened to that of two old friends, though we haven't known each other for long. When I first passed the threshold—and promptly tripped on a jutting wood plank—I was a nascent adult, overwhelmed by a life spent working and studying toward a goal that I'd held onto so tightly I couldn't see what it was anymore.

I had long discovered my life was waning, a little smaller and less vibrant each day. I didn't know what to do, so I had applied for a position teaching at a preschool in a small rural town. I hoped the increase in salary and vicinity to my family would give me the strength to make progress in a life that seemed so incredibly mundane that it had permeated something deep within, leaving me absolutely uninterested in the world.

The cottage needed repairs and a fresh coat of paint. It took months to recover it to a livable state. Looking back, the process was far more beneficial to me than the cottage itself. To take so much delicate care in fixing something, decorating it, and starting a little garden. To give time and love, even when you didn't know you had any left to give.

I began to film videos about my process of making a house a home, sharing both moments of bliss and hardship while living in the valley. I started with my iPhone before learning to use a proper camera. I posted the videos on YouTube and soon found similar souls that enjoyed my artistic take on rural life and love of storytelling. They supported the romantic nature of my short films. The videos were a way for us to stop, breathe, and get lost in dreamy rituals of tea drinking and nature walks and baking bread. They were a form of therapy for me, a reminder to focus on the beautiful things in my life and keep the rain clouds at bay. Those videos have changed my life and inspired my writing.

On my YouTube channel, I have shared how I seek out the wonder in the present. Also, the lessons I try and often fail to apply to my beautiful, ordinary, everyday life. The rhythms of slowness and busyness, resilience and hardship, patience, and gentle moments. The greatest thing that my cottage experience offered me was that I had never actually needed it. If one day I move again, if my life takes me back to my old city apartment, little will change. I truly believe that a beautiful life can only be cultivated through time and effort. It isn't so much dependent on where you live but *how*. The hardest lesson I have ever learned is that happiness isn't a location.

For so many years, I dreamed and planned and dreamed some more of my little imaginary cottage in the woods, far away from stress, worry, and unhappiness. But, as

The Cottage Fairy Companion

far as I know, things just don't work that way. In my naivety, I couldn't grasp that *you* follow yourself everywhere: your problems and fears and burdens. If there is only one message that I wish to convey in this book, it's that *you* are your home. Nothing else will feel right until you do. A dream achieved will quickly sour if you are not your best friend. My cottage never made me happy, and to this day, I am still learning how to be content.

I hope this book—a collection of prose, poetry, recipes, and crafts—will inspire you to look at your life more closely and notice the magic that has always been there. Those unassuming moments overlooked by many, patiently waiting to be rediscovered.

Spring

Busy days are good days,
when followed by quiet moments.
Sit for a spell
and remember why today
joyful or bittersweet,
is more alive
than any other day.

A Gentle Start

Spring will always be my favorite time of year. I didn't notice the change of seasons much when I lived in the city, which I now realize was due to a lack of observation. Even there, signs of spring were visible. The green tips budding from the trees, the way the air loses its frosty demeanor, giving way to something far gentler and inviting. I sometimes wish I could step back in time and relive those years more aware of the subtle, fascinating shifts in my environment.

Transforming my experience of daily life was a slow process. Not a grandiose change that happened overnight. Instead, it was a sweetness that seeped into my world, bringing a warming sense of purpose along with it. To spend the days with the goal of simply noticing a little more and hurrying a little less. It didn't suddenly change the pace of my life, as work and family kept me forever busy (as it does still). Instead, I began to invite my mind to not rush along with the pace of my body. To try to take a moment, when possible, to reflect on what the day has offered instead of continuously defaulting to worrying—or my phone—for comfort. How could I enrich my day and find those little moments of magic throughout?

I started this process by reigniting my imagination and a more "childlike" sense of joy. On an overcast day in April, I purposefully jumped in my first rain puddle in fifteen years. I got mud all over my boots and couldn't help but throw my head back and laugh at my own silliness. That same day I spotted a spider's web and became absolutely enraptured by it. The rain had left it a glittering maze of dewy fibers. Instead of simply noting the beauty and moving on, I now try to stop and absorb every detail. There is something indescribably healing in looking closely.

I had an insatiable fascination with all things fantasy and fairies when I was a child. Most evenings you could find me crawling through fields of clover and hiding behind tree stumps with a little insect net just in case I found a pixie frolic. What I intended to do with such a creature if I caught one, I hadn't the slightest idea. Having since grown a bit wiser, my obsession has been tamed and turned to learning the intricacies of nature—the rhythms of life and death among flora and fauna. As an herbal tea lover and *very* amateur forager, I've enjoyed the quiet hobby of learning how to respectfully utilize the plants around me: learning to enjoy the delicacies of nature while allowing them to prosper by taking only small amounts. I seek them out in forgotten corners of my valley where other humans do not tread. In the city, this had not been possible, so every year, I would take great joy in selecting my seeds to cultivate a little herb garden on my porch.

Whether you have limited access to nature or not, I think great joy can be found by considering how you might bring life into your home. I think this can be especially beneficial in the city, where there is less greenery and little that is wild and untamed. But this does not mean that you must live apart from the natural world, as it is still there—only in more subtle forms. It may be the tender shoots sprouting between sections of the sidewalk, a summer breeze, or the warm sun on your neck. The cycles of dawn and dusk, the moon growing and waning with such grace. There is so much available to be discovered in every environment. Perhaps a way to start would be with one small act of giving: growing a single seed to maturity, something hearty and robust such as a sunflower or marigold.

Seed-to-Flower: A Meditation for Intentional Living

Each spring, you will see a little flowerpot on my windowsill. It is placed there once the weather warms. You may not notice it if you enter my cottage, yet it is part of an honored tradition that I wish to share with you: Many of us have grown some sort of plant life during our childhood. Perhaps it was for a school project or simply out of curiosity. In my case, as a child, I would take a handful of sunflower seeds from my mother's bird feeder and plant them in little paper cups each summer. I would continuously drown them in water, no doubt more than they needed. Yet, every year, one or two little sprouts would appear. I would spend countless hours watching them, noticing the leaves unfurling ever so slowly. I cannot imagine finding the time to watch a sprout grow as an adult, but the memory has inspired me to grow a flower in a little pot each year and document the experience.

I encourage you to try growing a single seed next time the weather permits. Even if you are an avid gardener, treat this experience differently than you would the cultivation of a large plot. Keep this seed on your windowsill or an honored place outdoors, depending on the space available and the flower's needs. You will now take note of each step of the process of growth.

I always find it helpful to read up on the plant growth cycle, as it is endlessly fascinating. Sometimes I research the history and symbolism behind the plant I will grow (a surprising amount of old folk and fairytales are inspired by botanical life). For example, sunflowers (one of my favorites) are often associated with happiness and generosity. They also are preoccupied with the heavens, as you can see their shifting faces follow the sun throughout the day.

You find them alluded to in Greek mythology and in more modern stories as well. Knowing the plant's tale gives it meaning beyond the scientific name and its soil preferences. The sunflower is no longer just a sunflower; it is a living story that draws from countless years of human interaction and change over time.

Here is a suggestion of how to treat the meditative process of growth: First, I choose the seed I wish to grow. Usually, it is a flower variety that does not require much effort to flourish. Some hearty blooms that come to mind are marigolds, sunflowers, calendula, nasturtiums, and coneflowers.

Before placing it in the soil, hold the seed in your hand and think about something that you wish to grow in your heart. Maybe it is to grow in patience as you deal with a situation burdening your heart. You may be seeking healing or to grow in love and gentleness with yourself. Perhaps, you have something you have been holding on to for longer than you wish: pain, resentment, or sadness. While planting this seed will not resolve these feelings, it can offer a guide as you begin the journey. As the seed grows, you can see it as a process that reflects your personal growth. Take note of how your seed spreads its roots and needs water and sun. What do you need to strengthen your "roots"? What do you need to flourish? What steps can you take to nourish your soul?

Each morning you can take a moment to notice the progress of your seedling, allowing time for internal reflection as needed. Make observations in a journal, or simply reserve a little time in your thoughts to appreciate the progress you and the seed are making. Once the flower blooms, you can rejoice in where you are and in the beauty that abounds as a consequence of taking the time to set down your root system and acknowledge the vital resources around you. Once your plant begins to fade and wilt, see it as a release of any emotions you are trying to let go. Or a moment to consider all the inner work you have done. If you are religious or simply enjoy meditations or prayer, this is a wonderful opportunity to take time to strengthen your spirituality or simply get to understand yourself better.

Now that your flower is forming its seeds, consider the cyclical nature of your life. We will also bloom, wilt, and regrow throughout our lives as needed. Once the flower is completely dry, I usually take several seeds and store them safely, a small reminder that new beginnings are always possible. I plan to replant them when I feel so inclined and enjoy the cycle again.

Of course, this exercise will not cultivate personal or spiritual growth unless we allow it to inspire and guide our ability to connect with ourselves. The seed-to-flower is an opportunity to consider how we can develop and change and embrace the process. I have heard that phrase echoed by so many in my life when I've sought comfort: embrace the process. Everything takes time. Each flower grows differently, blooms at different times, withers, and goes to seed. You can never truly predict what will happen, but you can *embrace the process*.

Questions to Consider While Your Flower Grows

✦ Imagine you have a root system, much like a flower. Where are the roots? Are they in your mind, your heart, your entire body? Outside of your body? Where does your "strength" come from?

✦ What are your sources of nourishment? Apart from your basic needs, is there something else you need? Perhaps it is a few minutes alone with your thoughts each morning, reading a book, creating art, taking walks, etc. What is it, and how can you incorporate it into your life?

✦ What do you need to flourish? What steps can you take to nourish your soul?

✦ What other types of cycles can you notice within your life? What can the trends you see within your relationships, friendships, body, and emotions tell you about yourself? What wisdom can you take from them?

Working with Flowers and Herbs from the Cottage Garden

My favorite common flowers and herbs to grow are dandelion, lilac, mint, thyme, chamomile, and rosemary. All of these can be used to make delicious tea. Initially, I was unsure about what thyme or rosemary would taste like and was pleasantly surprised by the sweetness and lovely scent when boiled in water. Growing your food is difficult, especially if you have limited space or time. I find that growing flowers and herbs are so rewarding and require minimal effort, as they are content to quietly grow on a porch or windowsill.

My favorite flower for tea is lilac. An enormous white and purple bush grows outside my mother's house. They are such beautiful and bountiful blooms that attract wonderful pollinators. I enjoy the process of harvesting, choosing only one or two little bunches. I have made lilac simple syrup and lilac rice pudding, both deliciously rewarding experiments.

Tips for Harvest

Many edible herbs and flowers can be used in tea and recipes. When it comes to tea, I find my favorite sources apart from lilac are chamomile and rosemary. Even if these flowers are not as readily available to you, the options of flowers and herbs to use are endless. I often pair the dandelion and chamomile with a touch of honey. In addition, each year I love to experiment with using these herbs in a variety of syrups, jellies, and baked goods. Once you know how to properly harvest and dry each herb, you can get creative with its uses. I have included some simple recipes below.

You must do some research regarding all herbs and flowers intended to be used, as there are optimal ways to harvest each that can ensure the best taste and longevity of the plant. For example, I harvest dandelion leaves to mix into salad early in the year when the plants are still young and often less bitter than their more mature selves. When it comes to flowers, I always carefully remove the petals I intend to use from the stem and leaves. I also do not harvest flowers immediately after they bloom, giving them enough time to feed the visiting insects. Once learned, the process of growth and harvest will feel second nature and inspire you to be even more creative with your recipes.

Sustainability is the key to peaceful coexistence with both your garden and the wild world, and I encourage you to reach out to your local experts to learn about the intricacies of your local ecosystems (as well as invasive plants and how to deal with them appropriately).

Floral Simple Syrup

You can use this syrup for a delicious addition to drinks. I like to combine it with ice and sparkling water on hot days. You can also pour it over ice cream and pancakes or use it in place of honey for a rich, interesting, and natural touch to your desserts, sweet treats, and tea.

What You Need

4 cups flower petals (you can use dandelion, chamomile, lilac, or even rose petals for an attractive pink syrup)

2 cups sugar

2 cups water

Directions

1. Bring water and sugar to a boil in a saucepan. Stir until sugar dissolves completely.

2. Add flower petals and reduce syrup to a simmer until flowers are wilted, then take off heat. Depending on if you wish the syrup to be mild or strong, let sit and infuse (covered) anywhere from 3 to 8 hours.

3. Strain the petals out of the syrup using a fine cheesecloth to avoid bits of flowers in the syrup.

Lilac Rice Pudding

What You Need

4 cups milk (this can be substituted for nondairy milk or you can experiment with replacing a few tablespoons with coconut milk for flavor)

1 ½ cups white rice (cooked)

⅓ cup maple syrup or sugar to taste (I prefer maple)

3 tablespoons cornstarch

2 cups lilac blossoms

Directions

1. Simmer milk on low with lilac blossoms until blooms have wilted and turned brown, then strain out blooms. Now you have lilac milk.

2. Whisk maple syrup, lilac milk, vanilla extract, and cornstarch together. Slowly add white rice and mix thoroughly.

3. Bring to a simmer over medium heat, then turn to low for 15 to 20 minutes. To prevent the rice from burning at the bottom, stir often. You will know it's ready when the mixture thickens to a yogurt consistency and sticks to your spoon.

4. I find this rice pudding is best served chilled. A warning: The taste is very different from what you usually find at a grocery store. Working with nature will expand your palette in unusual and tasty ways.

5. Serve chilled or warm with lilac tea (a small handful of lilac blossoms boiled in 12 ounces of water). You can add more lilac blossoms to get a stronger flavor. The smell is divine.

Crafting for the Spring Cottage

As my favorite season, spring abounds with new life, laying the foundation for a fruitful summer. While my garden is mostly barren this time of year, the hearty wildflowers abound. During this season, I partake in a treasured ritual. I carefully tidy my home and enhance it with little decorations that remind me of the new light and life in my world. I love to use flowers and often decorate with any remaining dried stems I have saved over winter. I light candles that smell light and airy, spend more time outdoors, and try to bring any bits of color and vibrance into my home that I have missed during the winter. This usually involves collecting little fascinators I find in nature during my walks, newly uncovered by the melting snow. I make a lot of crafts this time of year, seeing every little effort as a way to establish my intention for the season: to welcome the renewal and growth of a vibrant spring.

Cottage Decorating: Flower Garlands

What You Need

A large needle

Waxed thread

Bunches of fresh or dried flowers

Hairspray or another adhesive spray to reduce shedding of blooms (optional)

Willow or other thin, long, and flexible stick (you can also use thick wire or rope)

Colorful ribbon (optional)

Directions

1. You can make a dried flower garland in two ways: either use only the flower heads (works well with roses and other flowers with many petals that hold their form) or bundle many small bouquets of stemmed flowers (my favorite method). This method is like making a wreath, another project I have included in this book. However, I think it is worthwhile to show multiple examples of how you can utilize flowers to decorate your home. Also, when it comes to garlands, the focus of the design is usually the flowers themselves. When I create wreaths, I often use a robust base such as evergreens or wheat to suit the outdoors. But when it comes to indoor garlands, you can use more delicate blooms.

2. Separate your flowers into equally sized bundles and then let them dry upside down in a well-ventilated area until they are mostly dry but pliable. This can take weeks, depending on how much moisture is in your flowers. I achieve the most elegant results by drying plants that have a delicate design that is not too dense and therefore easy to dry: globe amaranth, strawflower, cornflower, lavender, and statice, to name a few. To create a pleasing design, I suggest layering both long-stemmed plants with small flowers (such as yarrow or baby's breath) and larger, more statement pieces (such as coxcomb or rose). I use lavender and wheat in many of my designs as well.

3. If you are simply drying the flower heads for a garland, I recommend using a waxed twine to be able to adjust the flower heads once you pierce the needle through the back of each. After laying the flowers in the pattern you wish, take the strung needle and draw it through the back of each bloom (the base). If making a more intricate garland, I like to forage for a willow shaft and layer the blooms onto it, then hang it above my door or place it on a windowsill. If you would like a more flexible garland to hang on your wall, use a thick wire or twine.

4. To make a garland using bouquets, wrap twine around each bundle, making sure it is tight enough to hold the flowers in place as they continue to dry and shrink. Place your first bundle at the far end of your garland string, then layer the second one beside it to cover the stems of the first. Continue this process, taking care to "sew" the blooms together as you layer them so that they will not shift too much when handled. This is the most time-consuming part of the process. I also like to add ribbon and extra decorations as I see fit.

5. As with all nature décor, your garland will degrade over time. Garlands can become fragile and shed, so it is a process that must be repeated each growing season (I must admit, I like the idea that each year I will recreate my decorations anew. They are a little different each time). Spraying them with hairspray while they dry helps keep them together but is not necessary if they are displayed in a location where they will be allowed to exude their quiet beauty without being troubled.

The Cottage Fairy Companion

Collect Small Treasures

As a child, I was enchanted by the forest near my home and often brought back small treasures in the form of pinecones and sticks (I liked to think they were gifts left to me by the fairies). It was through revisiting this memory as an adult that I first went out and made a new collection of items.

My "box of senses" is now a yearly ritual. My partner once gave me a wooden chest as a gift. It is an antique with a brass lock. There I keep a small but thoughtful collection of objects. Currently, I have a pressed aspen leaf, a piece of tree bark, a green pebble with a soft indent on one side, and a piece of aromatic beeswax a local beekeeper gave me. In the past, I've kept a cone of incense or a small bottle of fragrant oil. These objects appeal to my senses and imagination. Also, they are often associated with distant yet treasured memories.

The unusual, jagged feel of the bark reminds me of a childhood spent climbing trees and reading books under the shade of an old pine. The sweet, roasted honey scent of the beeswax is particularly calming when melted under a flame. The leaf belongs to my favorite tree, the quaking aspen, and if I ever need to calm my breathing, I raise the leaf high above my head and let it fall, watching it spiral as I slowly inhale.

The pebble is my most treasured object from the box, found while wading through the river after a challenging workday. I had picked it up, choking back tears of fatigue, and held it up to the light. Still wet, the emerald undertones shone brighter, and I noticed the asymmetrical shape lent itself well to my anxious fingers. For weeks following, I kept it in my pocket and turned it over and over in my palm during stressful moments. Sometimes I'd run the tap and watch it transform from a dull, chalky exterior to a fresh green. That little stone always made my mind wander to a smooth, peaceful place. Full of sunshine and gentle water. It brought me to nature, no matter where I was.

I go to this box to reconnect with something simpler inside of me. I love to share it with children who visit, as they always have interesting observations to add.

It is a box of calming fears and worries—a box to remind me of a natural world outside my own, a world that experiences time completely differently, unaware of work shifts and overtime. A world where the only objective is to live. It is centering in a way, like raindrops on a windowsill, budding flowers on a riverbank, or a crackling fire.

How to Make a "Box of Senses"

I encourage you to try creating a box of treasures, even if it only consists of a couple of items. I find that the process of collecting these items is as therapeutic as returning to the box later. Something about the collection process always appeals to my inner child, helping me reclaim a joy and wonder that sometimes eludes me as an adult.

Some Ideas to Inspire Your Collection

✦ The senses: sight, sound, smell, taste, and touch

✦ The elements: Earth, water, fire, air

✦ The seasons: spring, summer, autumn, winter

✦ Your favorite memories, even if it is simply the memory of finding the object

✦ Items that calm anxiety: textured surfaces, items that help you feel grounded (I particularly like the cool, heavy feel of stones. I put many of my items underwater to examine them in different environments)

✦ Unusual-looking or shaped objects that ignite your imagination

Some Items You Might Collect for Your Box

✦ Dried flowers and leaves

✦ Candles

✦ Fragrant oils

✦ Stones

✦ Pinecones

✦ Seashells and glass

✦ Crystals and minerals

✦ Fossils

✦ Mini terrariums

✦ Incense

✦ Sand

✦ Moss

✦ Carvings

✦ Art pieces

I encourage you to go outdoors and see what catches your eye.

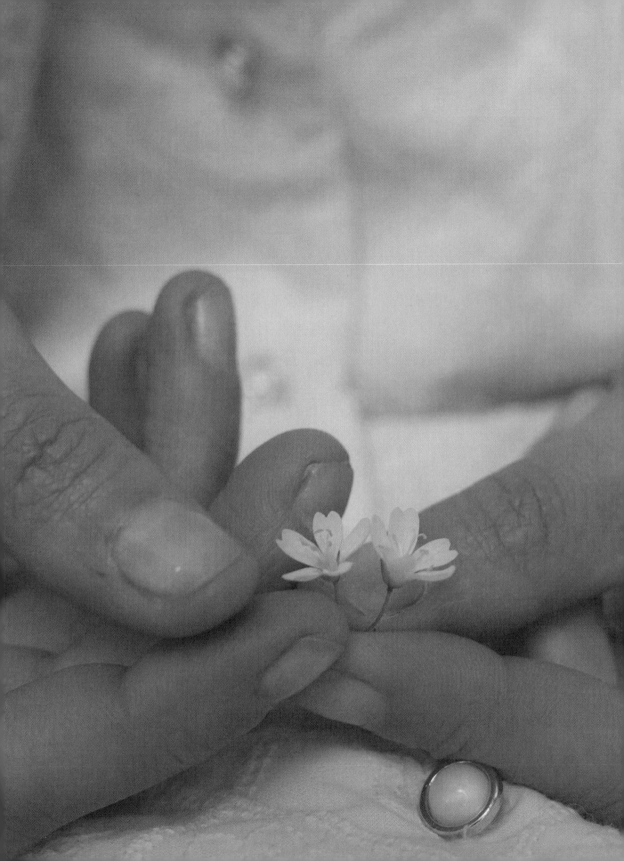

Experiencing the World Anew

Our five senses are constantly in use, yet we are rarely aware of more than a few at a time. When I feel overwhelmed or unsettled, I seek out a special place. My favorite haven last spring was a fallen tree two miles from my home. It rested overtop a little brook. I'd lie down across it and close my eyes, focusing on what I could hear. The pops and bubbles of the water, the squawk of the magpies, my own breathing made heavy by the trek. I would then reach down and let my fingers rest only an inch below the water, feeling its cool caress. There was not only a smell but also a taste to the air. It was hot and dry, yet the butterscotch scent of the ponderosa pine was there, light and sweet on my tongue.

I had a similar routine when I lived in the city. Through an observant eye, you'll notice little bits of nature everywhere. A shrub or tree, a delicate moth. Spring was my favorite time while living in the city, when the cherry trees bloomed along the boulevard, showering petals over the busy street. And when it rained and I couldn't leave my home, I would spend time with my houseplants.

Sometimes there's nothing more comforting than sitting in thankful awareness of our physical selves, our consciousness, and the ability to think and feel joy and pain. Our bodies and minds let us experience the world in our own ways, completely and utterly unique to ourselves. Our perception decides the meaning of the moment, our memory the value it will have going forth into the future.

In addition, I know many spiritual souls find great joy in developing a sense of the world outside of a physical experience, to go beyond sight and sound. If this is your wish, I will share that I have found great solace through letting go of my preconceived notions of the *right* way to pray or meditate. Strengthening your spirituality and intuition can be done in countless ways that don't necessarily involve sitting still in complete silence. While I love this traditional approach and have great respect for it, in my case, I found connecting to my spirituality became even more dynamic and alive when I realized that I could take meditative walks, sing, move, and create all while nursing that mindful awareness of the beyond.

Is there a pastime that makes you feel centered and at peace? Is there a way you can involve your spirituality in this process? I find stating your intention as you do a task can be quite helpful, letting your movements and thoughts flow, being open to receive and understand. Even if you are not spiritual, you may gain some self-awareness from stating your intention in what you do. For example, "As I sing, I am releasing self-doubt," or "As I walk, the feeling of my feet on the ground reminds me that I am whole, safe, and centered." Again, I think there is freedom in claiming your own form of spiritual expression.

A Little Gratitude Story

May is one of my favorite months. I love cool, crisp mornings on my porch with a good book. The sunrays peek through the drifting rainclouds and fall on my shoulders, comforting and warm. When I was a teacher, I would take my students to the riverbank this time of year to watch the salmon run. My youngest student was a little boy, barely four years old. During one of our outings, I found him sitting apart from the rest of the group. I walked over and sat down next to him. At length he turned to me and asked, "Have you thanked the world for turning today, Teacher Paola?"

His question caught me off guard. He continued to recount a documentary he had watched about how the planet turns on its axis, which is why the seasons change. We agreed that it was quite a fascinating and wonderful thing.

To this day, when things are hectic and I find my thoughts racing, I try to stop and thank the world for turning.

Beginning to *See* Again

The lupines are thriving, casting a delicate purple sheen over the valley. The sagebrush is growing again. Here it smells like fresh mint and sweet florals—it's distinct, a scent that always brings me home to myself, reminding me of who I am.

Today, I feel the need to cultivate peace, let go of my rushing thoughts and wander out my door at dawn. My steps are slow. A sketchbook in hand, I'm itching to create alongside nature.

Yesterday my mind was murky, leveled by unwelcome news and fears of a changing world. A seed of despair began to grow in my heart. Yet, in front of my cottage, a field of wildflowers is blooming. As I take a tentative step, careful not to crush the blooms, I fill my lungs with the heady smell: *columbia larkspur, scarlet gilia, a few lingering spring beauties*.

I wonder if today's experience could be enriched simply by seeing it anew. To seek soft shadows of wonder lurking in the trees, spirals of a curious magic in the clouds.

Unknowingly, that day I began a journey of sorts, one that regarded my interior life (a thing long retired from lack of use). Not a physical journey, but something far more adventurous.

I hesitate in my wanderings and simply look awhile. Right now, this valley is ripe with life. Scatterings of arnica dapple the forest floor. Low hills rise to meet the blue mountains far above the cumulus. Even from my position, I can hear nature whisper, "I'm still here; don't forget me." I realize that I love this place and that is what hope has always been. The act of loving.

I believe that peace of mind is not only achievable but grows in abundance once we begin to nourish it. I see it as a lifelong journey of letting go of unnecessary burdens, again and again, casting off the weight until—ever so slowly—the load lightens. If I ever find myself angry or frustrated, I like to go to the river and grasp a handful of sand. I lay my hand under the water and open it. As the sand is taken from my palm, I try to allow my feelings to flow. I always feel a bit better afterward and imagine this same process happening when I do not have access to water. Holding the emotion, accepting it, and then a slow release. As hard as it is, I try to remember to appreciate this feeling. Even if it is uncomfortable, it is also a gift, as difficult as that is to accept. My entire mind and body respond to this feeling, responding with energetic life. I am here, now, and able to experience this. An existence that is daunting at times but ever-changing. A time of peace will come, though perhaps not at this moment. But I know it will come, and in the meantime, I can choose to be kind to myself.

The Cottage Fairy Companion

I cannot speak for who I will be in my wiser years, but in my youth, I have found that happiness does not mean the absence of worry or pain. Instead, it's an acceptance of the cycles and strangeness of life, choosing to find hope where to others it may be hidden.

I have always been an individual with a dynamic range of energy. Some days I am filled with enthusiasm to make every day count, run wild in wheat fields, and speak to the skies. Other times I am subdued and sleepy, enjoying a cup of tea and a book by the window. The act of "making the days count" needn't be a static regime. Instead, it is an individual respect for the cycles of our minds and bodies. I do not always honor these cycles and resist living in balance with myself. I overwork, under eat, and live in the future. Consequently, spring is a special time for me. It is a season that invites me to recenter and rejuvenate. Spring is a time of new beginnings and miracles. We can take new growth as evidence that hope is a powerful thing. That we can always "begin again." Despite the bitterness of winter, seeds take root and the cycle repeats.

An Ordinary Pastime

Consider the passions you had as a child. Maybe it was art, music, athletics, building things, reading, baking, or dance. I encourage you to consider revisiting a lost passion for a day, even if it's as simple as finger painting, baking cupcakes, or running barefoot. Give yourself permission to partake in it without self-judgment. One of my favorite pastimes is making little baked treats while enjoying music or an audiobook. As an artist, I love decorating my creations and will easily spend ten minutes making a complex icing pattern on a cookie. If I look at my actions critically, the idea of decorating something that will be eaten in one bite not five minutes later is quite silly. But things we enjoy aren't always practical or rational. In short, consider letting your heart dictate an activity once and a while. It needn't be productive or useful; it can simply be.

The Winding Path of Healing

I moved to my cottage for many reasons. One was quite practical: I needed a job and wanted to be near my family. The other was more complex. I was recovering from an eating disorder and had become quite dependent on stimulants as a university student. I was a perfectionist, workaholic, and crippled with anxiety. I was everything I didn't want to be, yet I feared change.

A little girl existed inside my heart, sitting alone in a forgotten corner of childhood memories. She was a gentle spirit who wished for a life driven by curiosity, harmony, and simple joys. An explorer and wanderer, who wasn't so afraid of the world. I wanted to be her again.

The following years were a journey of learning how to be gentle with myself, to change my thought patterns and interior dialogue. I had to leave certain habits in the past and get back in touch with what made me, *me*. My body image had to be reckoned with. I had to develop a spiritual center and cultivate quiet courage to face the days and all their emotions. These are often universal struggles that we all face to some degree, yet sometimes—during a moment of fragility—it can feel as if it is consuming who we are. I invite you to consider what it is the makes you, *you*? This question may be hard to answer, and perhaps there is no real answer. But I believe there is worth in asking ourselves what defines us, what doesn't, and what we want to be. Is there a part of you that makes you uncomfortable to think about? If so, why? Is it your thoughts, body image, memories, or actions? What is the cause of that discomfort, and how can you take the first step in resolving it? I believe many of us hide from little parts of ourselves, the part that doesn't measure up to what we want to be. And yet, perhaps, addressing it is an opportunity to grow our intuitive wisdom. To face ourselves without fear, only to ask a gentle *why?*

As a lover of fairytales and a dreamer by nature, my path to healing was guided by writing and art. I tried to see my fears as the inevitable challenges all my literary heroes faced to fulfill their destiny. I read books. Many, many books. I began replacing destructive habits with healthier ones. I filled my life with color and plants and spent more time outdoors. I turned off my phone for weeks, letting my mind rest from an onslaught of advertisements and unrealistic standards of beauty. I faltered and found myself where I started several times. But eventually, I began to heal.

During stressful moments I still look at my past through a rose-colored lens and miss a time that—while painful—felt simpler. So many of my destructive habits came from wanting to control a life that is, in essence, uncontrollable. During my meditations, I divide the things I can control with what I cannot. Slowly, I began to accept that this was how things are. And that the unexpected is what gives life meaning.

Here are some questions I like to keep in mind on my journey. They help guide me back to my chosen path when I falter. The answer to these questions often changes over time, and I like to think that is a good sign. Maybe they will also relate to your life experience or inspire you to write some questions in a journal that can ground you when needed:

✦ What emotions/fears are you trying to avoid? What can you do to preemptively manage them better? What is one practical step you can take right now?

✦ How would you describe your soul to a stranger? How would you describe the color and texture? What activities make you feel in alignment with that part of yourself and most at peace?

✦ What can you bring into your day that will immediately improve your quality of life? What should you take out?

✦ What is a healthy form of escapism you can utilize? Painting, reading, cooking, movies, music, dancing, etc.

Many of us fear change in some shape or form. We may be excited to go on a road trip but fearful of leaving a relationship that isn't good for us. Change within our lives, the

The Cottage Fairy Companion

type that pushes us into the unknown, can be terrifying. It is a fear I have lived with all my life. Yet, I know that while you cannot control the future, you can have control over how you respond to events. You can cultivate fear or optimism. It is, and will always be, a choice freely made. And I also believe that to be optimistic is to believe in love, for yourself and others. Healing my mind and body had a lot to do with deciding whether I would continue to ruminate over my negative thoughts or celebrate the positive ones. To this day, I look into my bathroom mirror every morning and remember, "Your body is part of you, but it isn't all of you." And the people who deserve to be in your life will honor that universal truth. Change is a long and winding path to be taken with slow steps. If you rush your growth, you may stumble on that road more often than you wish. You must take care to observe your steps and trust that they will lead you to your destination.

Loving Others to Know Ourselves

I had never considered myself lucky in love. As a young adult I experienced a series of oppressive relationships that left me disillusioned and stubbornly single. When I moved to a rural town of five hundred residents, I accepted that my life—for the foreseeable future—would be one spent in the company of platonic friendships and family. I quickly came to see the worth in this and embraced it. I could have lived my entire life that way.

I eventually met a quiet, unassuming surveyor named Luke. The odds of this happening in a town of mostly retirees and families befuddled me. And he was there, real and gentle and endlessly patient. We are currently engaged to be married. The experience left me in awe of how unpredictable life can be. And how healthy relationships, romantic and otherwise, can offer healing. A popular saying I have heard time and again is that we cannot love other people until we love ourselves. But I wonder if that is true, because some of the greatest lessons I have learned have come from the triumphs and mistakes I have made in my quest to love another human. It is true that we need to have a healthy inner foundation to cultivate good relationships, but we cannot expect perfection from ourselves. The right people leave us raw and exposed in the best way; they challenge us to be better while communicating that we are safe and unconditionally loved. If there are only two things I search for in the people I keep in my heart, it is that they make me feel *safe* and *loved*. Everything else is an added benefit.

Whenever I begin a new relationship, romantic or platonic, I try to remember to question my intentions and how I feel. Perhaps they will relate to your experiences or offer guidance when you next allow someone into your life:

✦ Am I safe with this person? Physically and emotionally?

✦ Do I feel the need to "absorb" their needs, making their happiness my sole responsibility?

✦ Is my need to please them consuming my individual needs and wants?

✦ Is there room for "me" in this relationship, and is this person open to allowing me my freedom to express myself?

As someone who gains satisfaction from giving, I have learned that I also need to allow myself to receive. To be a constant "giver" sounds wonderfully virtuous, yet I don't believe this is true. I give my time and service to others because I want to, and yet often I cross a line where I begin to give because I am afraid of rejection or falling short of my or others' expectations. I don't see this as virtuous at all, and over time, my behavior can become a strange form of self-sabotage, disregarding my wants and needs for short-term gratification. I give so that I can avoid the questions of "who am I?" and "what do I deserve?" I don't expect this tendency to apply to every personality, as we each have our own love language. But I can assure you that if you are not this person, there are people in your life who are, and understanding the meaning behind our tendencies and loving expressions can strengthen bonds.

There must be balance in the energy we give and cultivate within. It isn't your responsibility to make others content, nor can you expect everyone to choose to include you in their lives. You can only offer love and accept the consequences, knowing it is better than not offering it at all. I encourage you to consider how you show love and how you receive it, and what that says about who you are. Love is an ever-changing landscape, allowing us to discover new layers when we least expect it.

Summer

Summer thieves wander the pine forest
and pluck the dew from open leaves.

The valley is flaxen and burnt brown hues,
but the mountains are always blue.

Cultivating a Loving Space

I didn't always value my home life. It was where I arrived each night, usually exhausted from work, ate a quick meal, and slept until my alarm buzzed the next morning. I was rarely diligent with the most basic of chores and was regularly overwhelmed by a mountain of tasks that needed to get done. I simply didn't feel that there was much benefit to creating a space I loved and that made me feel at ease. I didn't embrace cultivating a home that imbued safety and fueled my creativity and sense of belonging. I encourage you to consider how you can make your home a space that exudes the "feeling" you find most comforting. Maybe it is adopting a routine that gives you a few minutes to tidy each evening, or finding a space dedicated to creativity or mindful work. As for me, I find great comfort in having books in the house, always inviting me to sit down and enjoy a story, facilitating some moments for my favorite hobby each day.

I know it would have helped me during difficult times in my life, putting that little effort into creating a haven away from the stress of work and relationships to simply *be*. And to feel understood. To this day, I find great comfort in entering my home, seeing my paintings on the walls and books on the shelves, and knowing this place is a true haven for body and spirit.

When I first arrived at my cottage, I was faced with a miserably bare space. While I respect the spartan and practical home aesthetic, I prefer homes to feel cozy and be—while tidy—a place where I can keep things that are special to me. I like having craft supplies and paintings on the walls, a few select knick-knacks on the shelves, good smells, and a vase or two full of fresh flowers. I love teapots and bushy ferns and beautiful lamps. However, above all else, I adore furnishings and items that tell

a story. I enjoy items that are handmade, vintage, or upcycled. I didn't want to buy
new items for my home unless I absolutely needed to. I wanted to be a conscious
consumer and decided to seek out used items that would make my home unique. This
took time and patience. Two years later, I am still on the hunt for certain items—
particularly a reasonably priced table. My space has evolved into a home full of stories
and memories associated with how I found or made each item in it. I like it this way.
Through the process, my home taught me to be patient and to bring into it only what
I deemed useful or beautiful. I have always been frugal, and when an item seemed
far too expensive, I tried to learn how to make it myself. This taught me how to craft
home décor items by reusing thrift store finds or even foraging for natural art.

In my quest to create a space that suited me, I unleashed my full creative self on the
interior of my home. The hardest part was to cease worrying about what a visitor
might think of my taste. Once I finally let go of that notion, I began to paint on the
walls, drawing out branches and cherry blossoms and all matter of wildflowers. I
collected flowers and pressed them between glass frames. When lacking inspiration, I
listened to my favorite music and perused books on art and photography.

The key to creating an aesthetic space that I find interesting and wholesome was
embracing the slow process of finding items over the course of years and letting nature
inspire the rest. Rushed purchases rarely suited me over the long term, and over many
months of scouring antique shops I scored several intriguing items. I also discovered
the power of small cozy items, such as candles and floral bouquets, as a simple but
effective way to create the ambiance I enjoyed.

When you are decorating your space, I encourage you to sit and take a moment to
meditate on how you want to "feel" when you enter your home. What can you do to
create *that* atmosphere? Does it involve organizing things differently or reducing your
items? Is there a specific color palette that brings you comfort? Do you prefer warm
tones and soft lighting or more bright and vibrant energy?

An Ordinary Pastime

Make a list of things that you love and the memory of how each item made you feel. Maybe it's a beautiful song, piece of art, movie, or book that you truly love. An experience or location. Things that moved you beyond your ability to put into words, inspired your soul and dreams and changed you forever. In my case, I think about my first experience of Vivaldi's "Nulla in mundo pax sincera." I can equate this feeling to nothing less than true wonder at the magic this world can provide. It is a temporary feeling, much like a good belly laugh, and it reminds us that despite the problems our world faces, humans are still taking time to create beauty and share magic. Whatever is on your list, treat it as a special collection of things that brings you true joy. It can be a useful treasury to revisit when we need to add something extra to our daily lives, to reexperience something that reminds us of the power of being here, right now, feeling fully.

I take great joy in art and continue to seek it out daily. For example, during my nature walks I have begun to find the same intricacies of a Klimt painting reflected in the objects around me. I think, perhaps, as children we experience this wonder and joy more often than as adults—since we're still new to the world and all its fascinating elements. I remember seeing a butterfly wing under a microscope for the first time when I was fourteen. I gasped at the stunning intricacy and otherworldliness of the design. Since that moment, I've loved butterflies, and you can always spot some in my room. On another occasion, during one of my frequent walks, I found a patch of spongy moss growing on a boulder. Having brought a little ocular lens for this purpose, I took a peek. Through the glass I saw a city of life, layers of mosses and tiny green shoots and busy insects. It was a civilization no bigger than the palm of my hand. I could have just as easily passed it by without ever taking a closer look. At that moment, I experienced that beautiful sense of wonder that only appears when something is completely novel and inexplicably fascinating.

As we become adults, it can be easy to experience days, weeks, or years without moments of true wonder. By taking note of your experiences and observations, you can notice the magic hidden in the ordinary all around you. Of treasuring the list of beautiful things you wrote down, of using it to inspire discoveries. Of taking a moment each day to be still for a minute or two and be grateful for the mysterious inner workings of your body, of how you can breathe and think and love. I have again discovered a wonder in daily life through reclaiming the curiosity and daydreaming of my youth. This has impacted everything about who I am and how I live.

Living by Nature's Rhythm

My favorite aspect of my home is that the natural world inspires it. Leaves, flowers, pinecones—even the trees painted on my walls are a constant reminder of another pace of life. Nature reminds me of simplicity; today matters more than tomorrow, and to have shelter and sustenance is a gift to never be taken for granted. Most importantly, these elements remind me not to let the quest for efficiency and productivity rule my life. The practice of carefully utilizing your time is no doubt a virtue that can help improve your life—however, I think the definition of productivity should be expanded. Take time to laugh, invest in a relationship, give, sleep, and take care of your mind.

Our days are often governed by the clock. We are constantly aware of it from the moment we wake until bedtime. How we spend our time is of the utmost importance, many of us seek to "better manage our time" so as to not "run out of time." It seems impossible to live our lives without an acute awareness of the hours in the day, the minutes and seconds that so deeply affect us. And yet, there was a time when we didn't have a set twenty-four-hour clock. If we look to nature, we see that time—as humans know it—has a far different meaning. In the wild, time is divided into day and night, warm and cold, mating, feasting, and sleeping. There is time for everything, and everything takes its time. Yet for us, it is rarely that simple. The clock allows you to utilize every second of the day, potentially ensuring maximum efficiency and productivity. A quick search online will reveal thousands of articles on managing your time better, as if to waste any second is a tragedy—but is it? The turtles by my lake spend their time feeding, mating, and basking in the sun. They raise their young and prepare for the winter. There is time to do all these things, and their awareness allows them to follow a steady rhythm.

These days, I try to let my free time feel as fluid as possible. Maybe I don't have to be productive all the time. I allow myself time to "waste" time in the best way possible. Sitting in the sun, playing with my dog by the river. Enjoying quality time with a loved one. My lifespan, especially my work life, will always be deeply dictated by a clock. But not every moment needs to be that way. The time I get for myself, I try not to plan. I allow myself to simply be and forget the meaning of hours for a while.

At nineteen, I was in the grips of an eating disorder, an illness that dictated every minute of my day. There were minutes when I was allowed to eat and many more minutes I was not. My days revolved around time eating food and time not eating food. Spending time trying to distract myself, anticipating the time when I could eat. I was initially attracted to this practice to simplify my world, making the pressures I felt as a university student and young adult more bearable. Unfortunately, the practice harmed me physically and mentally, leaving me with complications that would take years to recover from.

Part of my healing journey was to let go of my obsession with time. Sometimes my body asks for food at an unusual time, or for a nap when I normally don't take one, or for a walk in the woods. Due to practical obligations, I cannot always honor these needs, but I try when I am able. I believe that I do not have too much time, nor too little. My life is exactly as long as it will be, and if I live it well, the number of days I have will not matter so much.

I invite you to choose an activity that brings you peace and benefits your mental health. Perhaps it is dancing, painting, hiking, or sewing. Turn off your phone or put away your watch and try indulging in this activity without giving yourself a set amount of time you are allowed to enjoy it. Listen to music or an audiobook, or enjoy the silence. Allow your body and mind to tell you when to do something else. I find this an interesting experiment that nourishes the relationship I have with my thoughts.

A Summer Story

My second August in the valley was, by far, the most challenging I have experienced. The first year the weather had been cooler than usual, chilly even. I was blissfully ignorant of how unusual this was and took for granted the rain in early September. That same time next year would be completely different. A heatwave followed by drought parched the valley, splitting the earth into a web of waterless terrain. The trees ached. Streams were reduced to a trickle.

We all held our breath when the storms came. After a childhood spent by the sea, I connected storms with heavy rain—but things functioned differently on the eastern side of the cascades. Thunder and lightning shook the canyons, but there was no rain. Bolts struck the trees, igniting flames that festered, waiting for a gust of wind to give it purchase.

The wildfires filled the skies with smoke, stealing away the sun for over a month. Firefighters, smokejumpers, even the national guard came, desperately digging fire-lines and evacuating locals. It was a terrifying time. My body grew to hold so much tension. My back and neck were in constant pain.

At long last, by October, everything had ended. The valley was quiet again, left to heal on its own. But I was still shaken, consumed by all that was lost. The animals, plants, trees…so many trees were gone. I drove out to the mountains the first day it was safe to do so and walked the affected forest, letting the ash fall from the charred branches onto my shoulders and hair. I stopped and sat, not bothering to put my coat down to avoid the soot stains.

I have great compassion for my past self but also pity. I was so absorbed in my sadness—in what I was convinced was a horrible event—that I forgot to ask questions.

I didn't ask the "why" and "how" of the situation. Why had the forest burned so readily? How does it recover? These questions may seem meaningless when faced with a dead forest, but I can assure you that is where the answers lie.

That same autumn I attended a lecture by a local naturalist. He sought to educate the locals about the wildfires, sensing there was lingering unrest and fear in his community. He showed us countless forest photographs, explaining how habitual wildfires cleansed the forest floors, delivering necessary nutrition to the earth and keeping the forests from becoming too congested. Fire was not only useful but crucial to keep the wild lands healthy. The transformed forest floor provided a new environment for animals, balancing the relationship between predator and prey, controlling numbers, and attracting species that preferred to live in such areas. He assured us that while it was still necessary to acknowledge the role of climate change, we also needed to understand how forest fires behaved and their natural place in the life cycle of the region. While fire scares us, especially when it puts our homes in danger, it is—innately—life-giving. It destroys select areas to preserve the health of the entire forest, takes away the homes of animals to ensure future generations have a functioning ecosystem in which to thrive.

This experience taught me a lot about how I process negative feelings. I saw the fires as a tragedy instead of seeking to understand the situation. I never tried to see things from the perspective of the wildfire itself. And yet, with an open and questioning heart, I could have handled that summer differently. There would have been challenges, and no doubt fear, but there had been no reason to despair. There would be new life, and with some courage I could have recalled myself to that fact every time I felt overwhelmed.

Fear is powerful. So much of our stress and anxiety is connected, on some level, to fear. But have you ever considered asking yourself why? Why does that fear hold such sway in your life? Could you adopt a different perspective or seek out information that would help you better understand your emotions? I believe that many of our fears are made up of layers. To peel back each one is to understand yourself a little better, to let it teach you something instead of controlling how you feel.

Now, when the fires come, I do not sit on my porch and watch the smoke clouds, ruminating on my fear. I prepare. I rake the dirt around my house, turn on the sprinklers, fill buckets with water, and leave out some for the thirsty animals. It is a methodical, practical approach. Nature is a majestic, healing entity—but it can be equally brutal, and that brutality must be respected. It is easier to believe a bad thing than wonder if it is truly as bad as we think. We must learn to stop, breathe, and seek to understand. Often, we are left in awe at the complexity of life.

Consider something that is a powerful source of fear to you: maybe it is the fear of death, or losing a loved one, a traumatic memory, a question about your life path or the universe. What exactly is it about these fears that scare you? Would you say any of these fears stop you from living the life you want? Do any of these affect your ability to freely love yourself or others? In my case, I have certain memories that upset me when they surface. I fear them because I have strong emotions associated with the experience and may even avoid spending time alone with myself in fear that I will ruminate. Yet, I have found great release in allowing me to encounter the memories fully at least once, to let myself feel everything. I have pounded a pillow, screamed at the top of my lungs, wept until my throat felt raspy and dry. Often, during it all, I feel a strange urge to laugh at myself. It is so rare we allow ourselves an environment where we can release emotions freely. Often, by the end, it feels like I got back in touch with an old friend, a piece of me that still believes life is beautiful. Bad things happen, and while the memories of those bad things may haunt us, only we can decide whether they will define who we are.

An Elemental Gift

Many people find that nature walks help alleviate anxiety and regulate breathing. For example, the sound of water—be it a seaside stroll or a babbling brook—can improve your mood only after a few minutes. I find myself particularly drawn to the river when tired or upset. I walk along the rocks barefoot, careful not to slip as I study the rushing water. I seek out a blue pebble, a green one, a heart shape. One that fits snugly in the base of my palm (a "worry stone," as a friend calls them). Sometimes I crouch and feel the glacial bite of the current wash over my hands. Surprisingly, I am often alone in my nature ritual. Runners and bikers pass through on a neighboring trail, heads downcast, breathing heavily as their hearts race. No doubt, exercising outdoors is a wonderful and enjoyable thing, but I am always surprised at the sheer lack of people simply sitting and looking, noticing little details that you couldn't possibly detect while rushing by.

One day, when I was focused on finding a worry stone, I spied a blue, egg-shaped pebble only a few feet away. It was perfect. As I reached for it, I saw a flurry of movement, scrunching my eyes shut just as a splash of water was thrown at my face. I lost my footing and fell, *plop*, waist-deep into the water. Tentatively opening my eyes, I saw I was face-to-face with a large wet snout. A golden retriever was inspecting me with concern, seemingly apologetic for his chaotic entrance. His mouth was slightly ajar, and between his teeth I could see the gleam of the rock. He was wearing a collar and trailing at the end of a threadbare leash was a little boy. He had been clearly catapulted into the water by his canine friend and was only now finding his footing while nursing a freshly split lip. He apologized, eyes averted, and I assured him everything was all right. We threw a stick for his dog and talked a while. We discussed our favorite rock colors and shapes, rejoicing at the rare finding of a piece of quartz crystal in the sand. While I enjoyed my solitary nature adventures, it was so refreshing to share the moment with an equally enthusiastic explorer. After a while, I bid them goodbye and started for home. Perhaps that little boy and his dog left a greater impression than I initially assumed, as only a couple months later I impulsively purchased a Labrador retriever from a man in a grocery store parking lot. A roly-poly creature with expressive eyes and an insatiable appetite, he would grow up to be a well-loved friend that would accompany me on all my future excursions.

Being "childlike" in our sensibilities isn't practical nor helpful as adults, when we are understandably expected to manage our emotions with more grace. However, I aspire to emulate every child's ability to seek out novelty in their daily life. I think there is wisdom in that wish to kinetically connect with the world: to throw rocks, feel the cold water, run your toes through the sand. As a preschool teacher I would watch as my students ran about the river's edge, exclaiming every time they spotted the exoskeleton of a naiad abandoned on the sand. It was such an exciting event, and even I had to admit the little papery bodies were fascinating and intricate. To this day, I make sure to visit the river at least a dozen times during the warmer months. I bring a book, a small magnifier, and a journal. I spend most of my time reading, but still reserve at least ten minutes to explore. I may give myself a challenge in the form of a scavenger hunt, or I may simply walk about with the intention of simply *noticing*.

Wherever you live, I encourage you to seek out water. Perhaps it is a small lake in a park, a rain puddle, or even a warm bath. It is an element full of mystery, a source of life and healing. Explore and experiment, much like a childhood fascination with cause and effect. Invite it to relieve the burden of worry. Let your thoughts be liquid and ephemeral.

My toes grow numb
as the trout skitter by,
bumping my ankles
with soft snouts.

The silken touch of true summer.

Crafting in Summer

In summer, I love my home to be a haven that offers refreshing serenity, something akin to the gentle sound of running water. I usually bring more bright colors into my home in the form of fresh flowers and summer fruit. I always have lemonade icing on the counter and citrusy, clean scents abound. I usually rearrange the furniture this time of year and utilize the coolest parts of the house more. I let the hard heat guide my day and am the most active in the morning and evening. If I can think of one thing that defines my home, art, and crafts in the summer it is flowers and plant life. Consequently, some of my favorite crafts for this time of year incorporate these elements.

Pressed Flower Art

Creating art with flowers is one of my favorite gifts and decorations. Collecting the plants needed is such a lovely experience, one that I love to share with children. The process of pressing and drying flowers requires patience and care, and the results are always attractive.

What You Need

Home-grown wildflower cuttings or leaves[1]

A clear and quick-drying glue

A glass float frame (pictured); you can buy frames specifically for pressed flower art

Either a flower press or parchment paper and a stack of heavy books

Tweezers

A microfiber cloth

A piece of paper cut to the size of your frame

Directions

1. First, dry your flowers. If your flowers are moisture-heavy (such as thick blooms or roses) they will be tricky to dry without growing mold or turning another color. Also, some white flowers turn brown as they dry. It will take patience and experimentation to find which flowers in your area dry best, but the most reliable method I find is by choosing already delicate flowers that have smaller blooms and are slightly dry (as are many wildflowers). You can also use leaves if you do not have many fresh flowers available.

2. To dry the flowers, you may use a flower press or sandwich them between two layers of parchment paper, weighed down by books. I recommend drying the blooms face down so that the petals spread out more evenly. Also, do not forget to dry stems and leaves (you can cut and

---

1 I do not recommend harvesting plants from the wild unless you live in a very rural place, as a small amount will not affect the health of the area. Do diligent research on the best foraging techniques: in short, never pull plants from their roots, only forage where there is little to no human activity and an abundance of the same plant, only take small amounts, and give thanks for the harvest.

dry them separately) as they can make appealing art. Drying flowers will take two to four weeks, depending on how humid your environment is.

3. Once your flowers are dry, carefully arrange them onto your piece of paper. I find creating your design on paper first and then transferring it to glass reduces potential fingerprints and pollen left on the glass.

4. Next, dab a small amount of glue on the backs of each piece and carefully place them on the glass. I recommend wiping down the glass with microfiber and using tweezers or gloves for this step. Let your design dry for several hours. If you make a mistake and place glue in an unwanted place, let it dry and remove it with a Q-tip dipped in acetone. Then wipe the area and polish with a microfiber cloth.

5. Once your pressed flower frame is complete, I recommend hanging it in a place out of direct sun, as heat can bleach the blooms. They make beautiful gifts and can be made in various sizes to use as coasters and ornaments.

6. Lastly, flowers naturally fade and degrade over time. While I have flower art that I have kept for several years, using natural preservation methods means they will not last over the long term.

Nature Terrarium Craft Project

Living terrariums are beautiful. I have a sealed jar with a little plant growing within. However, I can attest that it can be tricky to prepare the perfect environment for them to thrive. Since I still love the look of little sealed terrariums, I love to make mine full of what I like to call "nature's fascinators." Any little odd bits and bobs you've found in nature that speak to you. I love tiny pinecones and air-dried flowers. The options are endless, and I find the result can be truly darling and make sweet little nature-friendly gifts.

What You Need

Decorative elements are optional

A cork and bottle (I recommend a bottle wide enough to more easily arrange your items inside with your fingers or a tweezer. Also, a larger cork means more options for customizing.)

Colored moss (I recommend using dried moss, as anything alive or containing moisture will spoil. If you find some dried brown moss you can always add a bit of green color to it with dye or paint.)

A collection of items for inside your terrarium (tiny pinecones, stones, flowers, moss, leaves, paper with writing, etc.)

A small piece of self-hardening clay (You can use this to form a small mushroom to paint and adhere to the top of your terrarium. Feel free to get creative.)

Decorative ribbon and flower stems
Hot glue

Directions

1. Place items inside the terrarium. To emulate a living terrarium, begin with some dry soil, pebbles, and moss. They must be completely dry before being placed inside. I like to write some words on a tiny piece of paper and burn the edges. You then seal the terrarium and decorate the outside. I like tying a couple of layers of ribbon on the outside and gluing bits of moss, dried mushroom, or flowers to it.

2. Shape a tiny mushroom—or mushrooms—out of clay. I prefer polymer clay that you bake to dry, as the original shape is preserved better.

3. I like to put little written "hopes" in my terrarium (or "wishing terrarium") and give them to friends as little gifts.

Aloneness

There is a distinct difference between being lonely and being alone. One is a feeling, the other a physical state. A surprisingly effective way I began to cultivate peace in my daily life was to welcome aloneness. Also, choosing to use technology in ways that predominantly enrich my life and focus on what inspires and uplifts instead of feeding insecurities and negativity. When I first experimented with being alone with my thoughts, I found it challenging. Unwanted memories flooded my mind, regrets, noise. But this was only temporary, as I found that time spent alone doesn't mean simply being bored and in the company of intrusive thoughts.

I think we often admire those who can spend hours in silent meditation seemingly free of any need for external stimulation. While I am inspired by those who can do this, I have never been able. Perhaps I will someday, but in the meantime, I have come to believe there is no universally "correct" way to meditate. While I still try to take a few minutes a day to address some grateful words to the sky, my way of meditating is through work. My hands need to move, create, paint, and mold. My mind needs to have something to focus on, be it written words or music or ideas. It is when I am most creative that I am also most at peace with myself, when thoughts move through my mind freely without upsetting the balance. Also, I find that through this I strengthen my spirituality, another relationship that can only be cultivated through aloneness with one's own being.

I do not believe there is any one specific way to best connect with your spirituality, as we are all so unique and have equally unique ways to practice peaceful living. I can think of friends who feel most spiritual when on a brisk hike or run. There they feel most connected to their mind, body, and spirit. When I am amid an artistic storm of ideas—succumbing to the otherworldly portal of the imagination—I know who I am. I encourage you to explore your life and interests and connect with that inner voice.

I find that everything in your life is put into perspective when you are unafraid of yourself. Stress becomes less consuming, and relationships are connections that can be deep and meaningful.

I traveled to the coast two summers ago, aching to be reunited with the sea. My valley becomes crisp and dry in the summer, the prairie brittle and prone to wildfires. Even the broad lakes are not enough to appease my thirst for a lush and green world, and I yearn for autumn rains.

A family member had a little seaside cottage where I was invited to stay. I spent hours on their porch swing with a good book, nodding off to the sound of the waves on the beach. I spoke barely a word for two days, amazed that only a few years prior I would have been reluctant to spend so much time in my own company.

Loneliness is a feeling I used to experience often. I have found it isn't a feeling solely dependent on whether you have a lot of friends or an active social life. It's about your relationship with your spirit, fearing being alone with your thoughts, and missing a deeper connection with yourself and others.

I think most everyone feels "different" at some point in their lives. Often, we first experience it during our youth. These are times when we discover who we are, and it is natural that we feel like we cannot relate to a vast majority of people. We feel alone, like we don't belong.

Yet, the mere fact that this is such a common feeling shows us that isn't always true. There are thousands of books and videos and testaments about this feeling of otherness. It is proof that we have so much more in common than not at any given point. I've never been able to handle more than a couple of close friendships at a time, and I am quickly overwhelmed after several days of a lot of socializing. It made me feel like something was wrong, but I now know that many people are introverted like me; it's common. Similarly, some spirits are born more sensitive, tender, and introspective. Over time, I have found people that understand me and hold my trust. True to my innate shyness, those relationships took many years to build.

I have no doubt each of us has a unique light that wants to shine ever brighter as we grow in love for ourselves. We have individual imprints, but we also are more connected to others than not. I've come to see it as a responsibility to interact with my world with an open heart and accept others, assuming we share common ground. It has helped me feel less lonely and encouraged me to connect and give.

A practical way I combatted loneliness was by accepting that every emotion is an opportunity. I also had to let go of my pride and admit that in my case, I wanted to live my life near my family. In typical Hispanic culture, I was raised with a sense of constant togetherness. I missed that living alone in a city, and even though I was teased at times for wanting to be near my parents, I knew it would make me happier and less lonely. I have lived my life and made my decisions while still living near my family, and that worked for me. Through that, I realized how important it is to know your heart instead of mindlessly adhering to what someone else, or your society in general, dictates is the definition of success and independence.

I can certainly say that I still feel lonely from time to time. I think for some of us, it's a natural occurrence. But I don't see that loneliness as negative. If anything, it reminds me to value my spirituality and not take for granted the blessings in my life.

The quiet ones look on,
repose under the tumult
of an open sky—

At long last,
ready to believe
in the bliss
of a new day.

The Summer Kitchen

I find cooking to be one of my favorite pastimes for relieving the day's weariness and reminding me to be grateful for what I have. It's so easy to take small blessings for granted when we are tired, and something about the process of making food—such a simple and primal act—brings me home to what is important. I spend more time in the kitchen in summer, as there is such an abundance of options for ingredients. My garden is usually full of fresh fruit and vegetables, and so are the supermarkets. I spend more time cooking and enjoying the tastes and textures, and canning and freezing items that I wish to enjoy in the winter. I love lime and lemon this time of year, cold drinks and floral concoctions. It is a special time and a wonderful reminder to be grateful for simply having food. Consequently, it is crucial to share the abundance, and I find myself gifting much of the excesses of my garden.

Summer Flower Salad and Lavender Lemonade

I don't get too creative with my salads, as I like to keep my pantry stocked with simple, bulk items. However, what makes this salad specifically a "summery" salad is that I add edible flowers. For the most part, flowers have such a delicate taste that they are more for appearances than taste, but they provide a beautiful and uplifting look to salads, often taste like greens, and are a perfect centerpiece for dinners and parties. There are many types of edible flowers, but some of my favorites are viola, pansy, dandelion, nasturtium, daylily, and cornflower. Do your research and be 100 percent sure the flower you are growing is edible.

Summer Flower Salad

Few foods offer as much "liveliness" as a salad. Especially when I have grown and gathered the ingredients myself, it feels so satisfying to create and consume something so fresh and straight from the soil. The cool crispness of the leaves always energizes me.

What You Need

4 cups spinach or mixed greens

¼ cup sliced strawberries

Handful of sliced walnuts or pecans

Handful of crumbled Feta or goats milk cheese

1 tbsp of honey (warmed in the sun until runny)

Vinaigrette

1 cup edible flowers/ flower petals

Directions

1. I like to layer my salads to showcase the color and vibrancy as much as possible. I begin by tossing the greens and nuts and most of the cheese in a generous amount of the vinaigrette.

2. Placing them in a bowl, I add the top layer of flowers and strawberries and bits of leftover cheese and drizzle it with honey for that tangy-sweet taste.

3. I always serve it with lavender lemonade or another floral drink. If I'm feeling extra fancy, I freeze some violas in ice cubes for some added flowery flare to the drink I serve. Simple, sweet, and lovely to look at.

Lavender Lemonade

Add less or more of any ingredient depending on if you want a stronger or milder flavor

What You Need

4 cups of water

2–3 Tbsp sugar (sweeten to taste, using less if you prefer a tangier drink)

2 Tbsp honey

2 Tbsp fresh or dried edible lavender

Juice from a freshly squeezed lemon (use less or more depending on how mild you prefer)

Directions

1. In a saucepan over medium heat, bring sugar and 3 cups of water to a boil until sugar crystals dissolve.

2. Take the mixture off the heat, stir in honey and lavender.

3. Leave to infuse for 2 to 3 hours.

4. Strain the liquid through a fine cheesecloth.

5. In a pitcher, combine ice, water, lemon juice, and mix together.

The End of a Season

My feelings regarding each season vary. For example, I always mourn the end of spring, all too aware that the last wildflowers will soon wilt and dry under the hot sun. I can't say I enjoy summer in my valley; it is often tinged with anxiety over the unknown—whether or not the wildfires will come to our doorstep. But worrying over something that may or may not happen is fruitless. Indeed, I am certain there is no greater tragedy than a life lived in fear. We need courage to truly live and set our story in motion.

I experienced my first interior crisis shortly after I finished university. I had no idea what to do with myself. I felt burned out and disillusioned and terrified of the future. At the time, I didn't yet understand that even if you expect the world to offer you something, you may not find it. Slowly, I found my way, but looking back I see that I floundered for years, refusing to step out of my comfort zone. To admit that I was the only constant in my life—and that it meant I had agency. I took for granted the incredible privilege of deciding what to do with the time I had, a daunting task that can lead to indescribably lovely things.

I will never forget my first night at my cottage. I woke up in the early hours to the unsettling sound of coyote howls. Disturbed by the foreign wailing, I suddenly began panicking about my decision to move to the valley. I had made a horrible mistake. I had left my friends, social life, and a potential career in bookselling. I gave this up for a lonely cottage with a squeaky floor and condemnable plumbing. I barely knew anyone in town. My goals of being a writer and creative had been absorbed into the chaotic haze of my mind. This was not the last night I woke up in a cold sweat, fearing I was missing out on something important. And yet, each night it was easier. I could have saved myself many sleepless mornings by simply accepting that the answers would eventually come.

It's incredible how sometimes, by no effort of yours except patience and openness, the question of the spirit resolves itself. I found my way, slowly but steadily, without realizing it. The anxiety diminished, replaced by a conviction to find joy in my *imperfect* life and relief in how dreams can grow and mold themselves to fit circumstances. Understand that you have a lifetime to achieve your goals, and taking the scenic route to get there may have as much—if not greater—value.

During certain chapters of your life things may not be ideal, but they can still be fruitful. As your journey unravels, believe in the process. In slowness. In the power of intentional living and allowing the story to tell itself.

An Ordinary Pastime

I am a great believer in picnics. If you haven't gone on one recently, I encourage you to do so the next time you're near a natural area or hiking trail. A simple sandwich wrapped in foil and a thermos of tea will do just fine. It isn't an aesthetic picnic you are aiming for (though, by all means, wear a sundress and bring petit fours if your heart so desires), but simply the experience of taking a short journey and practicing gratefulness for a wholesome meal.

I usually take my little meal to a nearby brook or under the umbrella of a broad willow. I always bring a book, journal, or audiobook—depending on how I feel that day. Sometimes, if my mind is too distracted for reading, I listen to a story or quiet music. I relish the sun rays on my skin and take off my hat for a few minutes to thoroughly enjoy it.

When enjoying the outdoors, there is no single way to absorb it fully. Some days I observe with sharp eyes, spying little birds in the trees and cottontails grazing in a nearby patch of weeds. Other days I may keep my nose firmly planted in a book.

I truly believe that the benefit of spending time in nature is gained simply by being there. You are surrounded by life. In contrast to carpets and ceilings and home appliances, everything you touch is part of a vibrant network of green life. It is an environment well known to our ancestors, one that offers the gift of beauty freely.

Let me take you to a place
nestled among the mountain slopes,
where glaciers weep
as the birds sing.

You can find me with the dragonflies
disguised in a splendor of silver wings.
They flit and dive among the huckleberries
and make love in the grass.

The summer is nearly at an end,
yet my lips are stained and spirit light—
welcoming the sunset of the season
and dawning of the next.

Autumn

My dreams are like the tamarack trees,
glowing amber with needles of gold.

Under a hunter's moon
I dance with the dryads,
and they tell me their secrets.

The mountain slopes are vigilant
and so I become,
anticipating the frost
and diminishing light.

A Living Memory

In direct contrast to the anxious first days of summer, autumn fills me with excitement. The rainfall and cooling temperatures are a balm on my soul. August leaves me battered and worn by fears of smoke-filled skies, and come September, I allow myself a tentative sigh of relief.

Throughout the transition to autumn, I often think about death (and as morbid as this sounds, I do not believe death should be solely associated with something negative). Living in the countryside, I am faced with death nearly every day. I see the coyotes feasting on the remains of a recent kill, the ospreys flying low over the lake to grasp a jumping trout. The cycle of life and death surrounds me, and I count myself fortunate to witness this universal truth. To be ever more connected with how the natural world functions. It is a haven of beauty and grandiose vistas, but there is as much death as there is life here. And despite the violence, there is harmony and an acceptance that this is how things are. It has made me more interested in understanding death and resolving any uncomfortable feelings I associate with it. In that pursuit, I have found a growing peace of mind. It puts what I achieve in this life into perspective, making it seem far more important to spend my time creating precious memories and finding people with whom you can share love.

So much reaches the end of their cycle this time of year—or, at least, grows dormant in preparation for winter. A symbolic death, in a way. Everything that was budding with life in spring is now quiet and still. My nasturtiums are always the first of my flowers to be bit by a morning frost; one evening they are a congregation of perky orange blooms, the next they are a shriveled tatter of a former life. So many lives play out in this way, in the wild and human worlds. In my experience, when souls are taken suddenly it often hurts us the most, as we are the least prepared for it.

An old, cherished friend once invited me to dinner in their little cabin at the edge of a forest reserve. Not the type for casual conversation, they greeted me by stating that their firstborn had died the week before and that they wished to talk about it—if I would be so kind as to listen. The hours passed, and after the shedding of tears and a long embrace, my friend shared some words that I will never forget. I have tried my best to restate them in romantic prose:

> "We are living memorials to those we have loved and lost. Life may continue after heartbreak, but it will be innately different. And this need not be a sad thing. In fact, the experience can connect us to our souls more than we ever thought possible. It offers us a new life that no longer lives in the shallows, but left open and raw, ready to experience what this new world has to offer. The souls we once knew are preserved in stories written on our hearts, ones that we will recite again and again. And in that chanting of a memory, in bringing them back to life a thousand times over, we start to understand."

Already, I carry the stories of several people and animals I have loved. I suspect by the end of my life I will carry many more. And yet, I cannot be sure, because the seasons of my life are not laid out before me. I do not know how much time I have left, and while that can be frightening, I am comforted to know that it isn't up to me to decide. I don't need to feel pressure to make every day perfect and exciting and worthy of a final day on Earth; perhaps I only need to love.

Peace as a Practice

Since I started sharing videos about my valley online, I periodically get comments from unhappy people. They are dissatisfied with their lives and desperately wish they could move to my home and find the "peace" I seem to enjoy daily. It has always been a challenge to respond to messages like these, as I feel overwhelmed by everything I want to share and unable to summarize it concisely. I try to explain that I am not always peaceful. When I first moved here, I experienced the same anxiety and sadness that I had felt in the city. I was tempted to relapse into the throes of my eating disorder. Nothing changed, and looking back, I am amused that I thought something would. When your struggles are predominantly internal, they cannot be resolved by a new location. You cannot outrun who you are, but you can stop and try to learn to live with it. To seek the help you need, be it professional, spiritual, or—ideally—tapping into all the resources available to you.

As someone in the continuous pursuit of a peaceful mind, my motivation comes from knowing what it's like to believe it is impossible. I naturally tend toward racing thoughts, worries that keep me up at night with hand tremors and headaches. I am happy to report that these symptoms have lessened with time. I sought help but also embraced a journey of self-understanding. I now try to face my anxieties with acceptance and grace. To reiterate, peace isn't a location. I am certain of that.

Of course, not all problems are internal. Regarding difficult life circumstances, I must refrain from giving advice because no two situations are alike. However, I can share a bit of my story:

Two years ago, I lived in a condemnable apartment with a horrible rat infestation. The only window in my room was too small to use as a fire escape. More alarming than that, it was nailed shut—a fact I discovered after a drunk driver backed into our gas pipe one night and flooded the house with fumes. Thankfully, the firefighters arrived and put things to right. After that experience, I desperately wanted to find somewhere safer to live. Consequently, I needed to get a job that paid me more money. In a university town that only offered minimum wage customer-service positions, this was a daunting task. In my case, I was only twenty-two and blessed with a family willing to assist me in transitioning to a new job. A couple of years later, I was working as a teacher at a preschool and able to afford life at my little cottage. I was blessed to do things this way.

My mother grew up in poverty, and she raised us with knowledge of that reality, teaching us to cherish the privileges we had and recognize what had been sacrificed for them. The words I offer to those who feel like their current situation is not ideal are words she said comforted her continuously throughout her childhood. The sentiment has also guided me during challenging times: *We must believe that we are never alone.* For me, this is a spiritual phrase and applies to the physical world. Not all of us have families that can support us in times of need, but people are always seeking connection, stability, and love. Some families we are born with, and others we find. Each year is a chapter to a story not yet complete. Where you will be next season is not yet known, and while the present may be difficult, it can still be fruitful. You can gain something from this chapter and slowly but steadily build a new future. It may take months, years, or decades. Yet the journey can be worthwhile if we open ourselves to the experience and seek out the light.

Moving somewhere is never necessary to make great change in your life. If I still lived in the city, I would put more emphasis on my home environment and seek out more positive friendships while cutting myself off from people who influence me negatively. I would go to museums and free exhibitions, visit the library, and join a book club. I would be growing my balcony or windowsill garden (no matter how small)—even if I only have a couple of flowerpots and some low-light plants. I'd track the phases of the moon and sun and seasons, create a spiritual practice, and enjoy what little patches of nature I could find, even if that meant now and then taking a bus ride to a nearby park or lake. We can connect with our world and beyond no matter where we are; sometimes it takes a bit of creativity.

Shifting Your Perspective

A great horned owl lives near my home. He prefers to perch in a golden willow about fifty feet from my cottage. Occasionally, he observes me as I do yard work.

I remember when I noticed him one morning in early autumn. He was nestled against the trunk, eyes wide and fixated. I continuously glanced at him while collecting leaves. When I grew tired of work, I stopped and stood, staring back. Becoming uninterested, the owl extended his enormous wings and was gone without a sound. I was left with the memory of his strange eyes. There were countless centuries of wisdom encapsulated inside the body of that creature. His understanding of the environment we shared was so exact—a vast network of sights, sounds, and smells. Yet, I had pottered about for nearly two hours before spotting him in the trees. He had been acutely aware of my presence, and I had not known his. My awareness of my surroundings suddenly felt so basic. I thought of the countless mice and chipmunks that had scuttled by while I was distracted; the coyote observing me from a hillside a quarter-mile away; the quail

The Cottage Fairy Companion

sitting in her nest, hidden in the grasslands beyond my porch; the worms and beetles navigating the soft mulch of my compost bin. I knew all this must be happening, yet my senses failed to detect it.

We can experience so much in our lives, carefully examine everything we encounter, and still not know what it's like to experience the world as a life form other than ourselves. The thought reminded me of my smallness, how little we understand about the natural world we inhabit and the wild creatures that call it home.

My encounter with the owl inspired me to start climbing trees more often, curious to see things from the perspective of my feathered acquaintance. To compare, I would then lay my head on the ground, close one eye, and peer through the fronds of grass. It is, perhaps, a simple exercise, but I find myself drawn to it whenever I am anxious or ruminating over unwanted thoughts. The practice calms my mind, a challenge to consider things differently, to remember there is so much I don't know. It can be intimidating to admit that our knowledge is greatly limited, so much so that there is little we can be sure about. However, I am also comforted by the fact that it proves there is still so much mystery in the world, so much that is unknown. So many questions. So much magic.

If you have access to a garden or natural area, even a patch of grass, I encourage you to crouch down and consider it from an angle you do not normally utilize. Let your imagination wander, or—if you are trying to shift your thoughts to a peaceful state— imagine yourself as a small human. When I do this, I am reminded that the worries pressing on my mind would suddenly seem silly if I were only a few inches tall. A favorite children's author of mine, James Barry, once described little fairy folk as being "so small that they only have room for one emotion at a time." For a moment, I try to exist this way, the only emotions in my heart being wonder and awe at the detailed world existing under my feet.

Autumn Spiced Cider

An aromatherapy ritual

Something about frosty mornings and hot spiced cider go hand-in-hand, and while this recipe is simple, it is my favorite. Many recipes I have tried add extra ingredients: brown sugar, orange juice, bourbon (all these are options to enhance your drink). Others use prepackaged and dried mulling spices, which are also an option, though I find creating it from scratch incredibly enjoyable (and fresh orange rind has a delicious smell). The key ingredient for good cider is a simple, high-quality apple juice made from 100 percent fresh apples (not the concentrated or diluted kind). The juice is often murky or collects at the bottom (that's when you know it's the real thing), and the taste is incredible.

I treat the creation of this drink as a sort of ritual, to practice gratefulness for a new season and celebrate an abundant harvest. I can think of few recipes that involve such strong flavors and scents as spiced cider. It's an experience for all the senses. While you create this drink, take a moment to gently breathe in each ingredient. I personally enjoy looking into the history and folklore of each spice and understanding the grand journey they took to land in my kitchen.

What You Need

1 quart fresh organic apple juice	1 tablespoon fresh orange zest	Other spice options for experimentation: nutmeg, anise, lemon rind
1 tablespoon fresh cloves	2 cinnamon sticks	

(I like a *very* strong cider, so feel free to halve these ingredients if you wish for a more subtle flavor. You can always add more spices later!)

Directions

1. Heat over a stove at medium heat (allowing it to simmer gently, not boil) for fifteen minutes to an hour, as its flavor will mature and become stronger over time. It will also make your kitchen smell divine. If you heat

it for too long, the cider will become bitter—but do not fret! After it has cooled, add a bit of honey.

2. Once the taste has matured to your liking, spoon out the ingredients or run through a mesh sleeve. Garnish each cup with an orange peel, apple slice, or cinnamon stick.

3. I love serving this drink with ice cream and apple pie. You can always place the leftover ingredients back on the stove to simmer in water for the rest of the day, filling your room with festive smells. I've been known to leave my simmer pot out for hours.

Zucchini Bread

Part of recovering my relationship with my physical self (and celebrating what my body can do for me, not what it looks like) was nourishing it with homemade foods. Selecting your ingredients by hand and creating a wholesome meal is a powerful way to connect with the source of what you eat and connect with the plants and products you consume. It is taking time for your body and health daily and imbuing the process with love. This is one of my favorite recipes since it has a touch of sweetness and tastes incredible toasted with a dollop of butter in the mornings. The flour I use is from a local farm that grows highly nutritious grains such as Einkorn and Farro. While I do not expect these flours are accessible everywhere, I encourage you to get creative with the source of your flour, as some lesser-known varieties are as unique as they are delicious.

What You Need

2 cups Einkorn flour

¾ teaspoon baking powder

2 eggs

2 teaspoons of either cinnamon, nutmeg, or allspice (I combine a bit of all three)

½ cup brown sugar

2 ½ cups zucchini (grated)

1 teaspoon liquid stevia/sweet drops

¾ cup vegetable oil

1 teaspoon vanilla extract

Directions

1. Preheat the oven to 350°F. I use a 10-by-5-inch pan for bread loaves and line it with parchment so it doesn't stick.

2. Beat eggs, then mix all wet ingredients together.

3. Combine zucchini with dry ingredients. (If you want a less dense bread, place your zucchini in a cheesecloth and strain out excess water before adding it to the dry ingredients.)

4. Stir together both wet and dry ingredients until well combined, then pour into lined pan.

An Evening Meditation

I thoroughly enjoy crisp autumn evenings sitting on my porch, wrapped in a quilt with a steaming cup of cider in my hands. Last night was perfect for stargazing. It had been a cold and dry October day, and come dusk, the sky was clear, and I could tell it would be a perfect evening to watch for shooting stars. I was rewarded with plenty and spent the hours sipping away and trying to identify the constellations.

I encourage you to find a good place to sit this evening, perhaps outdoors or simply in a calm, clean space. When I was in the city and couldn't leave home at night, I would light a candle or turn on a star projector on my wall, letting my mind drift through galaxies for a while.

Once settled and comfortable, ask yourself a question. It can be any question, prompted by your wonderings, a book, or any tool you use for meditation. I often speak my questions aloud to myself, especially if it frightens me (as many do regarding my life path). The relaxing environment allows me to process the question and open myself to the answer. The only rule I put on myself is to address the question through a lens of positivity, consider *what if,* and use only gentle words full of hope. For example, I wonder, "How can I make the world a better place?" instead of "Why is there so much sadness in the world?"

Some Questions to Ask Yourself This Evening

✦ What makes me feel most content and satisfied with my daily life?

✦ What can I change in my lifestyle to encourage lasting feelings of comfort and security?

✦ What are the needs of my body and mind, and are they different from the needs of my spirit?

✦ How can I imbue more love into my day regarding myself or others?

✦ Am I balancing self-love with service to others? What can I do to regain harmony?

Healing the Bond

As humans we are dreamers. We tell stories, create art, and imagine other ways of living. For my part, I often find myself visualizing an idyllic world free of hate and prejudice. And rarely, if ever, throughout human history did we exist without feeding these darker aspects of our nature. I wonder why, then, can I so clearly imagine this perfect human world in my mind's eye if I never knew it? Why do I long to experience it with every ounce of my being?

While there exist a thousand rational explanations on why we dream of things that never existed, I often consider if at the center of our beings we are aware of an eternal wisdom, a harmony that is achievable if only we emulate nature. While the individual fight for survival in the natural world can be brutal, the bigger picture presents us with a different story. One of balance. Every living thing has a role in the cycle—they take neither too much nor too little—and thus peace is preserved. Ecosystems can thrive. As humans, we readily disrupt the workings of nature for our gain, yet claim to fight for a world that reflects the same principles of harmony. If that is true, then we are in dire need of healing. While we cannot heal that relationship for others, we can most certainly seek to connect with nature ourselves.

I know myself better
come harvest season.

It is a time for rosehips and morning dew,
when apple trees bend with swollen fruit
and squirrels gather their winter stores
alongside the autumn gnomes.

I taste the coolness of the days
on my tongue, and relish
the soles of my feet
on wet, mossy stones.

An Ephemeral Life

One of the hardest lessons my cottage insisted I learned was that happiness is, for most of us, a fleeting emotion. It isn't ever guaranteed to last. You may feel it for a day, a month, several years…inevitably, you'll find yourself facing a moment where you do not feel happy at all. Maybe you are grieving, feeling lost in your path, heartbroken, or afraid. You may feel a multitude of things, but happiness will not be one of them.

Only two years after moving to my valley I found myself working full time as an artist, a childhood dream of mine. I had a loving boyfriend, and we were excitedly planning a future together. And I would still wake up some days not feeling quite myself. Sometimes there would be a reason for it, a worry hanging on my mind or a stressful workday, but sometimes there wasn't. Often, I just felt *off*. I'd rack my brain trying to find how to snap myself out of it, to "think" my way to a cheerful disposition. But that didn't always work.

I thought: *Everything is going well in my life; why am I suddenly unhappy?* This filled me with horrible guilt of somehow being ungrateful for what I had. Yet, I believe that these less-desirable emotions naturally find their way to us from time to time. Perhaps it is a sign of a spirit that needs tending or the uncomfortable feelings associated with personal growth. Sometimes they are outside of our control or understanding altogether.

I am (currently) on a journey to finally accept those less-than-happy days after a lifetime of treating them like a disease I should avoid at all costs. Now I try my best to encounter them, gently accept that this is my current mood, and show myself extra love and patience. I believe there is value in respecting a periodic need to "go within" and remember to feed the spiritual soul, so often left neglected.

In contrast, the other challenge I face when I feel low is projecting it on the people around me. During a mental fog I may doubt the value of my job and the love of my partner and pull away from the positive things in my life, leaving ample room to entertain the negative.

If you are sensitive like me, perhaps you have experienced these "fogs" of sadness and negativity from time to time. It is a rewarding journey to learn how to face the gloomy days with the wisdom that few things last. While you cannot always be happy, perhaps you can also believe that your current feelings are not permanent. They exist in the present, but they do not define who you are or who you will be. You can find support if needed, and you can heal.

If there is only one lesson we can take from the earth, it is that nothing stays the same for long.

Wreath-Making and Decorating for Autumn

Decorating my home for autumn feels like a welcomed ritual, where I give my home a good clean and tidy, preparing it for the time when long dark evenings will keep me indoors. The tamaracks turn gold, poplars and birches transform from soft yellow to brilliant orange and red. I spend many hours collecting leaves for my flower press, waiting impatiently for them to flatten and dry. I then frame or use them in craft projects.

A favorite project of mine is making an annual autumn wreath. I find making wreaths to be very similar to flower arranging. Once you have a base, it's up to you to execute your vision. I love decorating with them in the fall and winter; it brings such a welcoming feel to the home. Wreaths have a rich history in many cultures, used for ceremonies and often worn atop the head as a symbol of status or festivity.

Making the base is surprisingly simple. I use several willow shafts and bend them in a circle, braiding them and tying the two ends together. However, you can also use bits of fallen branches, string, and hot glue to hold them together (it's okay if it turns out messy; you will cover up the base with your adornments). Another option is to find a metal base for your wreath at a shop or bend some old wire hangers into the form. The key is to have a strong circular base than can hold several pounds of decorations.

The next part is the most enjoyable, and that is going out to find your materials. A common material is evergreen branches, but you can also use wheat or dried lavender. Autumn is ideal for foraging decorations because many plants have dried out and gone to seed, so your wreath will not wither. It is natural for wreaths to shed a little, especially as they dry—that is one reason I tend to choose sturdy plants that are more likely to hold their shape. If the drying process is causing an unwanted mess, hairspray can help keep everything in place.

Common Plants I Use for Wreath-Making

- ✦ Evergreen branches
- ✦ Lavender
- ✦ Yarrow
- ✦ Fresh rosehips
- ✦ Pinecones
- ✦ Seed pods
- ✦ Wheat
- ✦ Bunched grass
- ✦ Moss and lichen

Following a similar process to making flower garlands, create many equally thick bunches of materials before layering them in a circular design, following the curve of your wreath base. You can use wire to bend around each bunch and hold it in place. Then, using a small string or wire, you can 'sew' extra details onto the finished product, such as bulkier decorative items like pinecones. Online you can find endless inspiration, or simply take a walk out in nature and see what speaks to you. I personally love the homemade feel of less perfect, asymmetrical wreaths. Do not be afraid to experiment!

Orange Slice Garland

This craft project never fails to cheer up my home this time of year. A touch of cinnamon essential oil will provide continuous good smells and a cozy atmosphere on candlelit nights.

What You Need

Orange slices (cut by a mandolin or by hand into no more than ¼-inch pieces)

A dehydrator or oven (preferably set to convection oven settings to help circulate steam)

Parchment paper (if using an oven)

Cinnamon sticks (about 12 or more, depending on how long you want your garland)

Essential oil (orange, vanilla, cinnamon, or anything else you prefer)

Thin hemp twine

Scissors

Dried lavender sprigs, mistletoe, pinecones, evergreen branches, or anything else that you want to use for decoration

Directions

1. First, dehydrate your orange slices—they must be completely dry. (Follow directions for dehydration based on your specific dehydrator.) If you do not have a dehydrator, you can bake the slices in an oven at 200°F for about 3 hours or more, until they are no longer oozing liquid. Flip the slices halfway through baking to evenly dry. No matter what method you use, the slices need to be 100 percent dry, or they will spoil. Be sure they are brittle to the touch before using them.

2. After the slices are thoroughly dried, dab a few drops of desired essential oil onto each orange slice.

3. To create the garland, cut your rope to your desired length, plus a couple of feet on either end.

4. Arrange your orange slices, spaced out evenly. You will now make a little loop of twine beneath each orange slice and poke it through the middle. Then slip a cinnamon stick through the loop, securing the orange and twine in place.

5. Do this for each orange slice. You may then add flower sprigs or any other decoration. You can tie these with thin wire, ribbon, or more twine.

6. Feel free to get creative. The possible variations on this design are endless. You can use lemon, lime, or grapefruit rings and decorate with numerous different types of dried plant life. I have used them as table décor during dinners as well!

A Question of Balance

My town has a small, one-room bookstore that I frequent. I enjoy perusing the shelves and discovering new stories. I remember one summer they received several different books about cultivating happiness and self-love. Intrigued, I sat down with a few to scan the contents. Quickly, I noticed that all of them had at least one chapter dedicated to the negative aspects of social media and how disconnecting from it has brought them lasting satisfaction. Now, I have no doubt this is true and am happy for the authors. In many ways, I can relate to them. After all, I am living in a cottage between two hills that block out all reception, and I rely on daily trips to a café to download the latest audiobook or show that piques my interest. Having been raised without personal devices, I had never been a heavy social media user. I used it infrequently and relied on in-person communications.

Once I started my YouTube channel, however, this changed. I had to use social media every day to respond to comments and upload videos. Initially, I found the work overwhelming yet found ways to manage it over time. My presence online led me to connect with other creators on various platforms. True to my interests, I soon followed updates on all my favorite book reviewers, historians, and crafters. I found their content compelling and was able to reach outside of my tiny town and connect with those who shared my more niche interests. Soon, I was enjoying correspondence with a fellow English major living in the UK, and even sent some physical letters back and forth. My use of social media added value to my life and led me to make some truly lovely friends. I have communicated with countless artists, mystics, and naturalists— some who I have met in person.

This isn't to say that I have an overly positive opinion of social media: I have read countless articles about how heavy use can leave us mentally tired and our self-esteem at an all-time low. It can lead to jealousy and feeling as if our lives cannot compare to someone else's highlights. Knowing this, I made videos on my channel about social media and how to disconnect when necessary. I understood how someone could feel their best without it altogether. But in each video I made, I always returned to a simple statement: Peaceful living does not entail eliminating things from our lives—instead, it challenges us to transform those things to serve us better.

Of course, this statement is not inclusive, as I can think of several former habits that most definitely needed to be eliminated to make me a happier person. For you, social media may be one of them. But I think there is also so much that we can enjoy better by improving our relationship with it. Instead of following creators who make me feel self-conscious or inadequate, I connect with people who inspire me. I limit my usage to the time it takes me to drink a cup of tea at my local cafe. I focus on what makes me excited to try new things, learn and challenge my thinking, or content that simply makes me laugh.

I have applied this same idea to several things in my life. One is food. As an incurable lover of sweets, over several years, I have reduced my consumption to the point that it has made me feel considerably healthier and more in control of my cravings.

However, I never eliminated it altogether and look forward to a small dessert every night. I relish every bite.

I also try to treat my anxiety as something that can live harmoniously within me instead of something I should spend the rest of my life trying—and failing—to eliminate. My anxiety allows me to cultivate deep empathy for others with similar personalities. It urges me to develop my spirituality and connect within and without and reminds me daily that no one can truly understand what someone else is going through. Despite the negative aspects of my anxious trait, it is a part of my life experience, and I try to treat it with a gentle hand. It is not a friend nor an enemy; it simply is.

I encourage you to consider the goal of "harmony" when transforming aspects of your life. Maybe the goal doesn't need to be eliminating anything and everything in your life that causes stress or discomfort. This is partly because—as far as I know—that is an impossible task that will leave you frustrated and exhausted. Instead, consider how your habits, routines, and relationships could be improved to enhance the simple joys of daily life. We cannot escape complicated and hectic moments, but we can learn to understand them better.

An Ordinary Pastime

Several years ago, I was gifted a book about words that were no longer commonly used in our vocabulary. Examples such as newt, larch, lichen, heather, osprey, and chicory. The lack of popularity of many of these words is understandable, as many of us do not live in natural areas where we observe a variety of flora and fauna on a daily basis. The book inspired me to check out some field guides from my library. I was itching to speak new words out loud. I studied photographs of mycotrophic wildflowers—a plant that shares similarities with both fungi and flowers—wanting to know what the namesakes looked like and understand how they existed in my world.

For example, yesterday I learned about the mysterious and rare flower known as the Sweet Pinesap. I had no idea it existed, and I found myself excited to bring it up in conversation the next time someone asked, "What have you been up to today?" Usually, I would answer with the generic "Not much" or "Ah, just busy." Instead, I exclaimed with enthusiasm: "I learned all about Sweet Pinesaps today! Have you heard of them before?"

Perhaps many people would raise an eyebrow at such an unusual response, but I think that's a good thing. To be actively learning—and sharing the joy of discovery—is such a beautiful part of the human experience, one in which we can all partake. No matter where you are, even if it's in an empty room, you can still discover something about yourself. When we go through our mundane routines day in and day out, it is so easy to exist within a bubble that does not stimulate our brains. We lose touch with the innate curiosity we once had in the world as children. By taking these daily opportunities to feed our interests and passions, we can preserve something that is otherwise forgotten.

Winter

I dreamed I was the wind and water,
sweeping over the mountains at twilight
as the cold settles in.

I dove and rose and dipped again.
I shivered the wings of birds with my fingertips.
I kissed the willow fronds,
leaving a glass castle in my wake.

I am the hoarfrost,
I am the sleet,
the snow,
the in-between.

I lay over a basin, moonrays on my back.
Changeling by nature,
I grow solid and strong

Quiet Living in Winter

It was -4°C this morning, a frosty reminder to skim the back of my closet for extra socks and gloves. As the solstice approaches, the days become unbearably short. I am restless and prone to a bitter attitude. When I feel this way, I find temporary respite by lighting a candle on my nightstand. I feed on firelight this time of year when the sun is so often absent. It's crucial to keep your thoughts focused on the light during such times. During all dark times, when our spirits are strained.

Maybe it's the long days spent indoors when blizzards rage, as December and January often make my body feel sluggish. It's as if the change of pace affects my perception of myself. As someone who values long walks on green hillsides, adventures on the river, and sleepy picnics in the sun, I find it hard to be as active in winter. It doesn't help that I have a low tolerance for the cold.

I go out on my Hok skis regularly and love my daily dog walks (bundled up to the point that I look like a well-fed caterpillar). Still, I spend far more time indoors, painting and reading. I enjoy it, but as the weeks stretch into months, I ache for the warmth of a spring breeze and grass between my toes.

Maybe you experience harsh winters where you live, or perhaps you enjoy a milder climate. Either way, I think many of us experience "seasons" in our lives that challenge us. If not related to nature's cycle, seasons of hardship and sadness in our lives that make the world seem a little grayer, daily activities harder to do, and our hearts heavier. It is when despair can creep up into your person, and carefree moments become few and far between.

It is during these darker "seasons" of our soul that it is crucial to focus on the light. To know that nothing stays the same for long and that brighter days are coming.

You are light,
You are gentleness
Though the world is vast
You are small,
and in that smallness take comfort.

Hold your light in the palm of your hand,
see it flicker with the beat of your heart,
feel your breath release,
and in the exhale,
rejoice in the many emotions of life.

Choosing Slowness

Winter in my valley is a time for slowness and coming home to one's inner self. A season for your body and mind to rest, live at a slower pace, and renew with the spring. Even if it isn't cold where you live, I embrace the idea that our body and mind need to "overwinter" and hibernate as necessary, healing from within to confront the new year (or a new era in your life) with fresh enthusiasm.

I find that winter is more challenging when we treat it like any other season. I often want to use my holiday vacation productively. Maybe I'll reorganize my home, make a new collection of paintings for my shop, or rush to find presents for friends and family. Yet, if we look to the animals, we see that their entire world drastically shifts during this time.

The wildlife around me has spent the greater part of the year raising their babies, gathering food, and preparing for the cold. Now that it has arrived, they rest and conserve their energy. In the face of a season so harsh and unrelenting, it isn't the time for the normal business and chaos of life. It is time to take deep breaths and rest when needed.

The Cottage Fairy Companion

Cultivating Resilience through Self-Care

My valley is home to the painted turtle. It is a stunning creature with red and yellow stripes. In the winter, they slow the mechanisms of their bodies down to the point that they survive at the bottom of the lake, under a layer of thick ice, for up to four months. During this time, they survive off their own bodies, barely needing air to breathe. Similarly, bears and chipmunks and all matter of animals prepare their shelters for a time of more sleep and less movement.

I try to apply the philosophy of my animal friends in winter. I have also begun to apply it to all cycles of my body. When my spirit, mind, or physical self yearns for rest, I try to allow it. Of course, I still need to work and go through daily routines necessary for survival. But in winter, I try to be even more respectful of my bedtime, putting my phone away and replacing it with tea and a book. Spending more time stretching in the morning, listening to music. I try not to let other people control my attitude, choosing to cultivate a sense of peace even when I am in a stressful situation. Winter is a wise season, reminding us of the importance of quality rest.

I invite you to consider some ways you can practice slowness this season. I find reading books about the behavior of nature and wildlife in winter is fascinating and attunes you to what is happening around you. Learning about the natural rhythm of my valley revealed a subtle yet intricate wisdom behind a world that relies on winter for survival. The snowbanks and ice and plummeting temperatures all work together to ensure an abundant spring. Maybe we are not so unlike these animals that we do not have anything to gain from also understanding the seasons and how they affect our lives.

The seasons will change,
and so will you.

Look to the cycle of the moon,
the wane and swell of water.

Tomorrow isn't spoken for,
and nothing stays the same.

Seek out the stars in your sky,
and on cloudy days
be as bright as the moon.

My First Winter

My first winter in the valley was difficult, as I was unaccustomed to such extreme conditions. I had committed myself to showcasing the beauty of my home through each season and sharing it with my subscribers. Through the lens of my camera, I had captured the delicate poppies of early summer, the grand sweeps of gold tamarack trees in fall, and now winter would be no different. But it was. Everything was so much harder. The legs of my tripod constantly froze in the snow and had to be dug out. After only a few minutes of fumbling with my camera's settings, my fingers were numb and red. The sweat on my face turned into painful icicles every time I stopped to rest. It was relentless. More than a few times, I found myself collapsed in the snow choking back tears of frustration. But I had to keep trying because more people were viewing my videos. They were finally being noticed, and while the future was as uncertain as ever, the one thing that I knew was that I wanted to continue sharing my valley. The sights and sounds, the seasons—including winter. I wanted people to connect with nature, care about preserving it, and see it as a teacher that could transform their lives. And with that conviction, I always found a way to pick myself out of the snow and keep filming.

It was worth it in the end, as the Methow winters are enchanting. I can only describe it as spiritual. The clear, cold nights of swirling star clusters are outright celestial. Then there's the groans and stutters of the lake ice underfoot, the hoarfrost coating the dormant willow in white crystal. Winter is a quiet yet powerful thing. It can transform a thundering waterfall into no more than a trickle, yet on a snowy morning walk in the woods the falling flakes make only the gentlest brushing sound on the tree branches.

Winter, above other seasons, makes me feel small. Maybe it's how, overnight, the vibrant hills of green sage turn into an endless sea of white. How the once inviting mountains are suddenly impenetrable under endless layers of ice. How I so heavily rely on my clothing and shelter to survive. The winter world is beautiful, but I am not like the rabbits and bobcats. I have no fur coat to protect my naked body from frostbite. During this time, shelter means warmth, and warmth is survival. It makes my existence feel rather fragile.

I have learned to embrace this feeling of smallness. It is far easier to wonder at the vastness of the world when you know how you fit into it.

Love and the Seasons

It was only my second January in the valley, and my YouTube channel had continued to grow. Soon, people all over the world were commenting on my videos. And with that, inevitably, came criticism. The comments that began to appear on my videos were predominantly positive and flattering, some critical and rude. The surprising amount of feedback on my appearance was strange and increasingly unwelcome. Even compliments were unnerving. The videos weren't supposed to be about me; they were about my valley, simple living, and storytelling.

My confidence faltered as my channel grew. Are my breakouts really that noticeable? Not to mention the finger that had been smashed in a door when I was a child and stayed stubbornly malformed. People were noticing things that I hadn't even noticed myself. I started feeling nervous about uploading my videos. So many people were watching, what would they say? Would I meet their approval?

Looking back, I can't help but laugh at myself. For a brief but challenging time, I had thought more about how I appeared in my videos than my passion for celebrating the beauty of my valley. Of living in alignment with ourselves and our world. The feedback had made me question my mission, the whole point of what I was trying to do.

I think we all experience moments in our lives when we feel deeply insecure and find ourselves fixated on our external selves. Maybe it's due to changes in your body, an unsolicited comment, or simply the mental impact of being surrounded by photographs and advertisements featuring people who don't represent reality.

If you ever feel insecure or negative about your body image, I wish to share how I challenged my insecurities. Firstly, I accepted that my body would change along with the chapters of my life. While I will always value my health and care for my body, the perception of others should not control my self-esteem.

To be truly confident you need to recognize that your body is the least interesting thing about who you are. Fill your life with laughter, adventure, art, and hobbies. Volunteer and nurture. Find value in your heart, your soul. Also, connect with your past and see the story of your people reflected in you.

I began to love my features again by delving into my ancestry and learning about my origin story. I am multi-racial and come from ancestors that originated in very different parts of the world. My people enriched their cultures with their personal stories. They suffered, and laughed, and told stories, the experiences of their lives reflected in the lines and shapes of their faces and bodies. I represent a melding of their features. By wishing to change a part of my body, I may be erasing a marker of where I come from, the story of my ancestry. For example, I was so insecure about my nose when I was younger. I also sometimes wanted straight hair. But now, I have really embraced both these things as representative of my mixed race, and I truly believe that by changing something, I'd take away what is so unique about my appearance.

I deeply encourage you to connect with your past and discover the stories of your people, wherever they come from. In every human narrative there is tragedy and resilience and rich storytelling. Embrace it and you are embracing the origin of the body you inherited.

The Cottage Fairy Companion

A Festive Kitchen

One way that I connected with my ancestors was by rediscovering my traditional cultural foods. This was a beautiful journey that reminded me how important it is to nourish your body with good food and the occasional dessert. It is so easy to rush meals during our busy days and choose convenience foods over taking time to prepare something special. I am guilty of this while working and know that often it cannot be helped. But learning to slow down the day in a small way, to really take time to prepare or eat food with patience and gratefulness is—I have found—profoundly therapeutic.

One of my favorite holiday treats is the traditional Puerto Rican Coquito. It is a drink that is often alcoholic but can also be enjoyed without the addition of rum. It is so rich that only a very small glass is needed, yet it never fails to make me feel cozy, sipping contentedly while wrapped in warm quilts and at the mercy of a good mystery book.

Puerto Rican Christmas Coquito

What You Need

1 12 oz can full-fat coconut milk

1 12 oz can evaporated milk

1 12 oz sweetened condensed milk

Vanilla, cinnamon, cloves, and nutmeg to taste

Optional: white rum

Directions

1. Blend coconut, evaporated, and condensed milk in a blender on medium for 5 minutes.

2. Add vanilla, cinnamon, cloves, and nutmeg. Add more or less cinnamon and vanilla to taste.

3. Optional: Blend in rum on a low setting for 30 seconds.

4. This treat is meant as a dessert to be served cold. It is traditionally presented in shot glasses as it is a very rich drink. You may bottle the coquito and chill it in the fridge for several hours before consuming; just don't forget to give it a good shake before pouring as the spices may slowly collect at the bottom.

Apple Maple Rose Mini Pies

When I think of festive foods, I can always taste the memory of cinnamon on my tongue. Cloves, nutmeg, maple syrup, apples, and pears are also holiday favorites. In early winter I usually get my hands on a few apples not yet spoiled by the cold. I recently got a mandolin cutter and enjoyed trying out new recipes using sliced fruit. My favorite is these simple yet beautiful tarts. They make such lovely gifts, and something about the delicacy of the arranged slices never fails to appeal to my inner artist. While I enjoy simple meals with staple ingredients during much of my work week, spending an evening baking something tasty yet beautiful is such a wonderful way to recognize the beauty in everyday foods. I enjoy this recipe because it can be adjusted depending on whether you want a sweeter dessert or simply want the more subtle apple/maple flavor to shine through.

What You Need

4–6 apples (I often use Red Delicious, but you can experiment with more tart varieties if you wish)

1 cup maple syrup

Standard pie dough

1 tsp. cinnamon

1–2 tbsp. brown sugar (to taste)

¼ cup butter

12-slot cupcake pan

Directions

1. Cut apples into uniformly thin slices, preferably using a mandolin. Slices should be thin enough that they are flexible and bend when held by one end.

2. Carefully lay out all your slices and sprinkle with cinnamon. (You can add a dash of cloves or nutmeg if you wish.) Then coat them in maple syrup. (You can use a pastry brush to ensure they are evenly coated.)

3. Place slices in a bowl and allow them to soften for 10 to 15 minutes. At this point you should be able to roll them up without breaking them (handling them gently, of course).

4. While apples are softening, roll out pie dough and form the shells in the pan (I like to add a braided crust). I brush each with butter and sprinkle generously with brown sugar.

5. Form the "rosettes" by carefully placing the slices in each well, overlapping each piece and working from the outside in. Optional: Sprinkle with more brown sugar and cinnamon if you wish, and extra maple syrup.

6. Bake at 350°F for about 30 minutes until the crust is lightly golden and apples are easily pierced by a toothpick. The bake time can vary depending on the thickness of your slices, so keep a close eye on them. Serve warm with vanilla ice cream, whipped cream, or simply an extra spoonful of maple syrup!

Note: You can always use puff pastry instead of pie crust for a more buttery flavor. I love having these for breakfast as they are sweet but not overwhelming. I can dribble some extra maple syrup over it if I want added sweetness. This recipe keeps things simple, but you can always add extra fillings. The possibilities are endless!

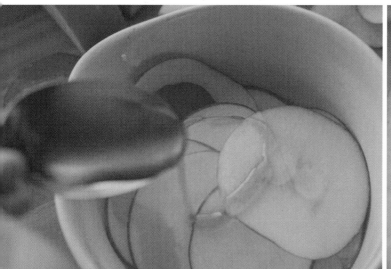

You Are Worthy of Living a Beautiful Life

The first "true" snowfall usually comes in December. We may have sprinklings that melt away in autumn, but by the end of the year my valley is buried by several feet of snow that stays put until spring. When I first laid eyes on this wintry scene, having only lived at my cottage for half a year, I remember being in awe of the abundance of plant life that so readily recovers from such an extreme season. How so much is under that thick blanket of snow, waiting to grow again. It made me wonder what I have buried underneath, what I have hidden away underneath the layers of my consciousness. What I want to uncover in the spring, what I want to keep tucked away. What I am afraid to see, to accept about myself. Maybe we all have mountains inside us that stay snowy all year, covered in glacial ice. Our forever winter, a little corner of our souls full of memories and feelings frozen in time.

I rarely meet someone who hasn't gone through an experience that challenged them on a deeply emotional level. Maybe it is a traumatizing event that requires a lifetime of healing or a period of emotional turmoil brought on by loss, abuse, anxiety, or stress.

These experiences transform our lives, challenge our perspective, and allow us the opportunity to offer compassion to others and ourselves. Sometimes, when we carry guilt or pain associated with these events, it can leave us feeling broken and aware of our infallible nature. We may have fallen short of our standards and beliefs and now carry it as insecurity. Maybe you have been convinced, however temporarily, that you have little value or agency.

I think that many sensitive souls struggle, at times, to feel worthy of certain good things. Maybe it's believing you are worthy of self-love and forgiveness, worthy of a healthy relationship, of feeling at peace with yourself on a regular basis. I never thought of myself as someone who feared happiness until I began to notice my own tendency to embrace anxiety and stress whenever the opportunity arose. I would barely try to calm my mind and automatically give in to panic. I *wanted* to feel stressed, because I didn't know what else to do with my more tumultuous emotions. On a subconscious level, I didn't think I deserved to feel otherwise. My body didn't deserve proper food and rest. I wasn't the person I wanted to be, and by default that made me a bad person. This fear was buried deep within the ice layers on my mountain. I knew it was untrue, yet I felt it was.

To learn how to manage my emotions in a healthier way seemed impossible because I believed it was. Being constantly critical of myself was something I found familiar. To go through life feeling generally content was frightening. It meant facing the part of me that caused me grief, seeing my flaws and somehow, despite it all, saying "yes, but I still deserve to be happy, to love and be loved." And acting on that statement, accepting the goodness and light. Of unloading the layers of winter, of accepting the warmth of a new season.

I encourage you to consider what you wish to renew for the next season, and perhaps what you want to let go. Is it believing you are unworthy of accepting goodness into your life in all its shapes and forms? What do you fear is true, what do you know isn't? Perhaps there is something you can alter in your life to more readily accept that goodness. Is your internal dialogue unnecessarily negative? Maybe it is your external dialogue, the conversations you entertain, that need to shift into something new. Words have so much power, both what is spoken and withheld. When we know what needs to be said and what needs to be released, maybe then we can begin to thaw and prepare for change.

The Winter Cottage

Living here in January, surrounded by open fields, has transformed my understanding of the coldest season. This time is crucial for the success of everything. The layers of ice melt to feed the ground, letting plants take seed. The low temperature regulates the number of animals who survive each year, harmonizing the relationship between predator and prey. The spring waters fill our wells. The rivers swell and the salmon run. Winter guarantees new life in spring. Winter is water.

In the city, I saw water as something that came out of a tap whenever I needed it. I wish I had seen its true value at the time. I took baths for granted and expected hot water in my teacup every morning. I observed the snow from my cozy and warm apartment, barely going outdoors. Interaction with the season felt limited compared to experiencing winter in my valley, but it didn't have to be that way. Nature is everywhere, even in the city; I just hadn't yet developed the curiosity to notice it.

Winter in my cottage forced me to interact with the season in far more uncomfortable ways. My home has a furnace that often blows a fuse during the coldest days of the year. I spent many a frozen evening trying to get it working again, watching my houseplants shrivel as the temperature in my home plummeted. Multiple times, I had to turn off the old pipes and lug in water in buckets.

Of course, I have much sweeter memories of winter. The rotund quail visit me often, looking for any bits of seed left behind in my flowerpots, their little bodies effortlessly skimming over three feet of snow. On my walks, I regularly spy bobcat tracks in the powder. As a lover of the winter holidays, I adore decorating my home. My favorite crafts are making wreaths, candles, lanterns, and garlands. Apple juice, cinnamon, cloves, and orange rings bubble continuously in a pot over my stovetop. I suppose it's the challenges of winter that make a warm and festive home more inviting than ever.

Lantern Home Craft

I rely heavily on candles and firelight this time of year. When everything is so dark, the brightness of electric lights can often give me a headache. Once the sun is down, I light only a small lamp by my bedside and several small candles. I am sometimes anxious to leave candles lit for too long as I am quite forgetful, so I equally enjoy battery-powered tea lights to accompany the copious amounts of apple cider I drink during the cold months. To decorate my imitation candles, I love to make paper tea light holders. They last several seasons and are some of my favorite decorations in my home, especially since they are easy to make. You can only use imitation candles in these lanterns, as they are flammable.

What You Need

12 ounces of basic washable school glue (Elmer's will do; this glue must dry clear or mostly clear)

12 ounces water

Several sheets of tissue paper in your desired color(s)

A large flat paintbrush

A rubber balloon(s)

A clothespin and string

Dried and pressed flowers, leaves, or paper cutouts

Small twigs and twine

Directions

1. Firstly, blow up your balloon to the desired size of your lantern.

2. In a bowl, pour glue and add one tablespoon of water at a time until the consistency is soupy without being runny. (A slightly thinner glue will be easier to use, but if it's too watery it will break the tissue paper. I suggest making a small batch and testing it until you find the best consistency. Test it by putting some glue on your paintbrush and running it over a small piece of tissue paper. If the paper breaks apart, it is too runny. The paper should absorb the glue and become wet without falling apart.)

3. Rip the tissue paper into strips.

4. You will now begin layering strips of tissue paper onto the balloon and painting over it with glue, using your flat paintbrush. One strip at a time, until three-fourths of the balloon is covered. Then hang up the balloon using the clothespin and string in a proper place to dry.

5. When the balloon is dry (this will take several hours or all day), add another layer and dry again. At this time, you can begin placing dried flowers between the strips of paper as you form your lantern (you can also wait and add your flowers under the last layer of paper if you wish for the colors to be more vibrant). You will then continue adding layers of tissue paper to reach your desired thickness. I recommend about 3 to 5 layers of tissue paper. Too thick and it may begin to look uneven; too thin and it will collapse.

6. Making this lantern will take several days. I have gotten quite creative with colors and pressed flower designs.

7. As these lanterns have round bottoms, you will have to create something to hold them upright. You can buy holders or make one out of layering three twigs in a triangle pattern and tying them with string.

8. The finished lanterns can be decorations as is or hold little electric tealights to add to an atmosphere of warmth and coziness.

Icicle Ornaments

Now, this must be the simplest yet most rewarding craft I have ever made. The epitome of eco-friendly art, it lasts as long as the temperature is below freezing and is beautiful even as it melts away! If you live in a cold climate, you need to try this out. (It is a great craft for children as well!)

What You Need

A silicone mold in any shape you wish (I used a 9-pan silicone mold for soap rounds, but you can use a Bundt cake or wreath mold, pretty much any mold you can find made of silicone! Intricate resin molds work as well, if you want to make an easy "ice sculpture" to display. Silicone makes it easy to remove your item once it is frozen.)

Water

A collection of natural treasures: anything from evergreen branches, citrus slices, cranberries, holly, leaves, moss, dried or pressed flowers, seeds, sticks, etc.

Electric drill with 1.4-inch drill bit (size depends on size of ornament)

Decorative ribbon or twine

Optional: natural food coloring (if you want to make "stained glass" ornaments)

Directions

1. Fill the molds with water and place your items on top, arranging them as you wish. Make sure each item is at least partially submerged in the water so that it stays in place.

2. Then leave the molds outdoors to freeze overnight or put them in your freezer.

3. Once thoroughly frozen, drill a hole into each ornament large enough for your ribbon of choice. I hang up the ornaments outdoors, where I can see them through my window.

As they melt, they grow clearer and catch the sunrays. Sometimes I fill them with bird seeds and get to watch the chickadees pick away at them. I never fail to get compliments when people see them. The process can be repeated throughout winter and the leftovers are composted for the spring.

An Ordinary Pastime

For me, winter is a time to connect to the past. It is an excellent season to light candles and revisit the stories of your ancestors. I find that connecting with the lives and legends of the people who came before can be very centering when faced with the uncertainty of the impending new year. Despite hardship, tragedy, and unexpected events, our ancestors lived on—finding comfort through the bonds of love and friendship, wondrous tales told by firelight, and the taste of homemade food.

I have several books on history, mythology, and folktales that I use for this very purpose. It is not uncommon to find me huddled next to a wood stove this time of year, wrapped in a tartan shawl, reading the legends of the Arawak and Celtic people. I encourage you to venture into the history of your ancestors this winter—you may be surprised by what you find. In a reality where we are so often made to feel unworthy due to our gender, race, or background, I think it is crucial to take pride in who we are and where we come from.

> Within you is a story
> tended by your people
> and knowledge greater than your own.
>
> Listen, and you will remember an ancient word,
> passed on by those who came before.

Conclusion

If I could describe living simply in one phrase it would be "elevating the ordinary." It is the practice of transforming our daily experiences and finding meaning, purpose, and beauty in everything we do. We are allowed to take occasional breaks from the more stressful aspects of life to breathe deeply and exist *differently* for a while.

The greatest benefit I gain from looking at life this way is that it relies on embracing a more positive and hopeful outlook. After working as a teacher, I know that our little people are looking to us as an example of how to handle a future that feels uncertain. By showing them that we need to seek out the magic and be the artist of our own lives, we can make lasting change. And our life story becomes a legacy of not only what we did, but the people with which we connected.

We need to understand our reality, to experience the tragedies and heartache. We must know them fully and ask ourselves how we can help. And then we must know how to dream, to imagine a better world, to seek out the goodness. The love. And in that act, we uncover something innately kind. A peace that exists not from lack of awareness but from bridging the divide. Maybe I'm an idealist, but I wouldn't want to be anything else.

I will continue to pursue a gentle life. And I hope that this book has offered you, at the very least, some moments of reflection. A reminder that life goes up, down, and up again. It is complicated and chaotic, and gentle and sweet. It breaks and mends, flows and falters. And in the midst of it all, you take a moment to wonder at the beauty and notice that the mundane never really was. And you have something within you that no one can ever take away.

About the Author

Paola Merrill is an artist and storyteller based in rural Okanogan County, Washington State. She spends her time working at her local bookstore, creating YouTube videos, running her Etsy shop, and reading books. A lover of nature since birth, her work seeks to bring awareness to the untamed beauty of wild areas and inspire others to protect the wonder. She believes that some of the most beautiful lives lived are rarely talked about and that there's a little sacred child in each of us that wants to be understood. After getting married she will be moving out of her cottage and onto a new adventure in a forest home. You can find out more about her journey on YouTube @ TheCottageFairy.

Etsy Shop: TheCottageFairyArt
Instagram: The_Cottage_Fairy

yellow pear 🍐 press

Yellow Pear Press, established in 2015, publishes inspiring, charming, clever, distinctive, playful, imaginative, beautifully designed lifestyle books, cookbooks, literary fiction, notecards, and journals with a certain joie de vivre in both content and style. Yellow Pear Press books have been honored by the Independent Publisher Book (IPPY) Awards, National Indie Excellence Awards, Independent Press Awards, and International Book Awards. Reviews of our titles have appeared in Kirkus Reviews, Foreword Reviews, Booklist, Midwest Book Review, San Francisco Chronicle, and New York Journal of Books, among others. Yellow Pear Press joined forces with Mango Publishing in 2020, both with the vision to continue publishing clever and innovative books. The fact that they're both named after fruit is a total coincidence.

We love hearing from our readers, so please stay in touch with us and follow us at:

Facebook: Mango Publishing
Twitter: @MangoPublishing
Instagram: @MangoPublishing
LinkedIn: Mango Publishing
Pinterest: Mango Publishing

Newsletter: mangopublishinggroup.com/newsletter